'Spa... ...oir . . . D... ...s off quite a feat in managing to w... ...ctingly, yet ...ll wittily, about her unspeakable grief . . . lea... you smiling and with a lump in your throat'
Mail on Sunday

'A touching and life-affirming memoir . . . a thoughtful glimpse into bereavement and a celebration of the undoubted healing power of pets'
Max Pemberton, *Daily Mail*

'You will cry as much as you'll laugh. A must-read memoir'
Cosmopolitan

'[Emily] writes with verve and vigour, and you will be rooting for her'
Sunday Mirror

'Emily is both searingly honest and funny, and ultimately gives us hope that things can always get better'
Heat

'Funny, sparklingly honest and heart-breaking'
Bel Mooney, *Daily Mail*

'Funny yet heartfelt'
Red

'A wonderful and very special book that made me squeak with laughter and had me in floods of tears'
Adam Kay

'Both very funny and moving, Emily Dean's writing will make you laugh, cry and stroke your dog (or any dog)'
Sarah Millican

'Heartwarming and heartbreaking all at the same time! Genuinely couldn't put it down'
Alan Carr

'Incred... ...tten. I urge everyo... ...nk Skinner

LO...BOROUGH ...ARNET

D0774317

Emily Dean is a writer and radio presenter. She is Frank Skinner's co-host on the award-winning *Frank Skinner Show* (Absolute Radio) and currently presents a hugely successful podcast for *The Times* called *Walking the Dog*. She spent eight years as Deputy Editor of *InStyle* magazine and has written for titles such as *The Times*, the *Evening Standard* and *You* magazine. She lives in London, supports Arsenal and her career highlight was when Mark Gatiss called her 'sci-fi royalty' due to her childhood role in BBC cult series *Day of the Triffids*.

Everybody Died, So I Got A Dog

Emily Dean

HODDER

First published in Great Britain in 2019 by Hodder & Stoughton
An Hachette UK company

This paperback edition published in 2020

1

Picture, p. 96 © Michael Testa, www.michaeltesta.co.uk

A CIP catalogue record for this title is available from the British Library

Paperback ISBN 978 1 473 67138 6
eBook ISBN 978 1 473 67139 3

Typeset in Sabon MT by Palimpsest Book Production Ltd,
Falkirk, Stirlingshire

Printed and bound in Great Britain by Clays Ltd, Elcograf S.p.A.

Hodder & Stoughton policy is to use papers that are natural,
renewable and recyclable products and made from wood grown in
sustainable forests. The logging and manufacturing processes
are expected to conform to the environmental regulations of
the country of origin.

Hodder & Stoughton Ltd
Carmelite House
50 Victoria Embankment
London EC4Y 0DZ

www.hodder.co.uk

To my sister Rachael – for everything xx

I think it is only fair to tell you that I was devoted to your mother. I owe my very life to her. She was brilliant, beautiful, and loyal to the end. I shall always treasure her memory. To you, her daughters, I pledge my friendship, forever and ever.

Charlotte's Web, E.B. White

Contents

Prologue

This is a story about losing an entire family and gaining a dog. But you've probably worked that out already. As spoiler titles go, this one is up there with that film *The Assassination of Jesse James by the Coward Robert Ford*. If you want to tell the unvarnished truth, though, I reckon you should do it from the very outset.

I didn't know that my journey back from loss would involve dogs. They had always been symbols of a life I'd longed for but never had. I couldn't have predicted that a crossbreed called Giggle and a Shih Tzu who looked like the star of a film called *Chewbacca – the Early Years* would change everything.

There are certain things you have to accept in life. No good ever comes from a sentence beginning, 'I hope you won't take this the wrong way . . .' One day, the people you love will no longer be here. And you'll probably die without ever really knowing how to pronounce the word 'furore'. But, perhaps it's never too late to try and get your shit together.

When you wake up one day with nothing, in a sense you have everything. What if you could start your life over again?

Part One

Treacle

Chapter One

We would never be a dog family. It was Cookie Monster who made me realise that.

The epiphany came while I was watching his performance of 'One of These Things', the lighters in the air hit of *Sesame Street*. Something about his cover version spoke to me. He really made it his own. As his ping-pong eyes bobbed about wildly, contemplating four plates of cookies, he delivered the words that would stay with me for the rest of my childhood. 'One of these things is not like the others, one of these things just doesn't belong! Can you guess which thing is not like the other thing? Before me finish me song?'

He didn't have to finish me song. I knew already which thing was not like the others. It was my family. Because the others were dog families. And we would never be a dog family.

People with dogs represented every aspect of domesticity that was right and functional. We represented everything about family life that was curious and unpredictable. Those people with their spaniels, their setters and their terriers inhabited

EMILY DEAN

another country – they simply did things differently there. I longed for a dog, desperately, passionately. But not as much as I longed for us to be a dog family.

Dog families gave their children something called 'tea' at around 5.00pm. When my older sister Rachael and I went to friends' houses, their mums would produce Marmite soldiers, fish fingers or Findus beef Crispy Pancakes and orange squash. We would then be ushered into a room with a pastel floral sofa and yucca plant, to watch *Blue Peter*. The dad's plum Ford Sierra would nose into the drive around 6.30pm and a Collie or a Labrador would race to the door to greet him. 'Hey you, how's my good boy!' the dad would say, ruffling a furry neck. The dog would lick the dad dutifully and the whole family would settle down to watch David Attenborough's *Life on Earth* before bedtime.

Dog families set aside money for phone bills and insurance policies and cleaning products and food for the freezer. We existed on overdrafts and loans, which went on black cabs, first editions and paté from a posh shop called Fortnum & Mason. Dog parents taught you how to ride a bike. Our parents gave us masterclasses in deconstructing poetry, opening bottles of wine and charming bailiffs. And if the children in dog families asked, 'Why is Granny being horrible to me?' the mums tended not to respond with, 'You know why, it's because she's on AMPHETAMINES, darling.'

In the unlikely event dog families got a parking ticket, they paid it before it escalated into court appearances. They ate Rice Krispies before school, not the melon and Parma ham starter from last night's dinner party. They didn't use letters

6

marked 'Final Demand' as wine coasters. They didn't forget to mention that the Sex Pistols would be filming in your bedroom today. Dog families punished you for misdemeanours by sending you to your room or withholding your pocket money. Not by sticking a series of handwritten Shakespeare quotes up on cupboards. 'This above all: to thine own self be true' or more hauntingly, 'Cowards die many times before their deaths.' And dog-family car singalongs didn't generally kick off with a song that began, 'Sit on my face and tell me that you love me . . .'

For the first seven years of my life we moved between houses, schools and continents with the casual indecisiveness of someone idly surfing TV channels. One moment we were living in a Victorian mansion flat in Battersea, the next a wisteria-covered cottage in Surrey, suddenly a wooden bungalow in New Zealand, then a modern beach apartment in a northern suburb of Sydney, before transferring to an Art Deco flat overlooking the city's harbour.

We witnessed a boat capsizing on our first day in Australia. 'Darlings – HIGH drama!' cried my mother, as my parents woke us up and ushered us on to the balcony to watch a rescue crew drag what was left of a man's life ashore. 'Shark attack!' my father informed us, guiding us through reports on our new marine neighbours in a *National Geographic* magazine. Two weeks later my parents were telling friends over midday carafes of wine how 'extraordinary' it was that we'd shown such reluctance to get in the sea. 'We even hired an Olympic coach!' they said, with a shrug. Perhaps shark-gate was their subconscious way of connecting us with the essence of our own existence, as we moved through life like Great Whites, torpedoing between friendships, houses and schools, bouncing frenetically from 'So sad you're leaving!' cards to 'Welcome to your new home!' tags attached to poinsettias in empty rental houses.

It was a lifestyle that required ambassadorial levels of charm, resilience and portability to carry off. 'The itinerant Deans!' was the cry with which we were often greeted in the book-filled houses of our literary friends, uttered by dads in paisley shirts as mums smelling of woody Seventies fragrances struggled to rescue lunches ready two hours previously. We came; we gave great anecdote about my father's career as a BBC arts reporter and documentary maker – 'Michael, tell everyone about when you interviewed Barbra Streisand!' 'Did Gore Vidal really try to seduce you?' 'The Duke of Windsor documentary was simply wonderful!' then, often pursued by taxmen, we disappeared.

Shortly before my seventh birthday and just after Rach's ninth, after eight homes, three countries and seven schools, my father gave us a taste of domestic stability. He had fallen hopelessly in love with a magical nineteenth-century folly in north London called Holly Village. My mother hurriedly enrolled Rach and me at the local primary school, which was filled with the glorious progeny of dog families.

The house was decorated with mossy gargoyles and turrets, and wreathed in ivy. Our landlords, like everyone to whom we owed money, were shrouded in malign mystery, but I knew them as 'The bloody Walkers.' 'Don't write on the walls, girls, remember the bloody Walkers!' 'They want the rent again, those mean bloody Walkers!' I had never encountered the enigmatic 'bloody Walkers' but I imagined them as hooded figures running skeletal fingers down an inventory of comments like 'Fag burn on nylon duvet', written in scratchy Gothic script.

So under the haunting gaze of Karl Marx, our formidable stone neighbour in nearby Highgate Cemetery, we settled into life at Holly Village. I got to know its alcoves and ancient Bakelite telephones, the smell of damp and the Victorian larder filled with Dijon mustards and gourmet preserves in place of the Pedigree Chum tins and family-sized Ribena bottles favoured by my school friends' mums.

The house had only two bedrooms. 'Well, technically three, darling!' my mother insisted, of a spider-infested turret crammed with old costumes and wigs, manuscripts of abandoned attempts at plays and theatre programmes. There were also scrapbooks filled with newspaper cuttings of my father's TV appearances. Before his move into documentary reporting, he had been one of the rotating hosts of a BBC arts discussion show called *Late Night Line-Up* along with the broadcaster Joan Bakewell. It was the kind of show where men with vast sideburns and women in knee-high suede boots smoked and argued into the night with playwrights, philosophers, artists and actors. The job had filled our address book with literary names such as John le Carré and Doris Lessing and given my father the unanticipated honour of being the first man to appear on British colour TV – a moment probably lost on the seven dusty academics watching.

My parents' jobs were mystifyingly absent from my book *What Do People Do All Day?*, which featured animals happily engaging in human professions. There was a walrus wedged into dental nurse's scrubs. A jumpsuited raccoon tinkering underneath the chassis of a car. A rabbit in cabin-crew uniform welcoming a fox on to a plane. But I couldn't see any dad bears in floral shirts, cigarette in paw, chatting to Germaine Greer about gender politics. And there were no mummy pigs draped in silk kimonos on garden loungers, applying sun tan oil under a speech bubble that read, 'Darling, get off the phone, my agent might be trying to call.'

'My agent might be trying to call' was a phrase Rach and I heard a lot when we were growing up. Followed by my father conspiratorially whispering to us with amusement, 'But alas, he never does.'

My mother's acting career had been derailed partly by the arrival of first Rach and then me, but also by my father's addiction to relocating, which explained the slightly erratic nature of her credits. 'Is your mum famous?' friends would ask throughout our childhood. 'She played a Turkish brothel owner in a police drama,' we'd reply, to blank looks. 'A corpse in *The Adventures of Sherlock Holmes*? She was in a Tampax ad?' We would watch our peers' interest dissolve, as their dreams of introductions to the man who played Danny in *Grease* collapsed.

Not long after our return to England my mother began to dabble with bouts of understudying in West End theatres. 'Right, just off to break a leg, girls!' she would announce, zigzagging down the stairs of Holly Village in strappy heels and snug designer jeans. She would envelop us in vast scented hugs as she left, perfumed with bergamot, tobacco and exotic adult otherness. This was Nighttime Mum, the one who commanded smoky dressing rooms filled with boisterous actors, who flirted gently with the Stage Door man and urged her colleagues to have 'just another glass, get it down you!' Daytime Mum wasn't like that. She insisted we have ballet lessons, took us to art galleries and cooked *coq au vin* the way my father liked it. Daytime Mum smothered us with soap-scented cuddles and soothing 'there there's' if we were sick. The two characters seemed to be stuck in an eternal tussle.

My parents encouraged Rach and me to immerse ourselves in my father's work, so we would stay up late to view a studio debate about the morality of cosmetic surgery or an interview with a literary giant, sleepily trying to make sense of questions such as 'Doris Lessing, have you always found yourself sitting in judgment on your civilisation?' as we curled up alongside my sister's ever-present Rupert Bear doll. Rupert, like us, carried the travel scars of a hardened foreign correspondent, having accompanied Rach across the world. He was her most treasured possession. Perhaps Rupert's appeal lay in the fact that he always returned safely to idyllic village life after his adventures, a denouement less easy to lay bets on in our storyline.

Rach was consistently drawn to representations of a gentler, bygone time. She collected period costume dolls and concealed her conventional beauty with an Old World eccentricity. Even her entry into adolescence would eventually be heralded not by slamming doors but by honking Handel on her trumpet in the bathroom every night, locked away from the commotion. My interests were generally more brash and peer-endorsed. I collected infant status symbols – a Chewbacca notebook, a Paddington diary, a TV-advertised memory game called Simon, that announced your defeat with a dramatic bass tone. But Rach had no desire to be like anyone else. She didn't share my longing to be part of a dog family. She regarded our family life with good-natured grace.

Her view of me was similarly tolerant – the exasperated love of an indulgent parent who wheels out euphemisms like 'spirited' to excuse questionable behaviour. 'Emmy, that's a silly-billy thing to do,' she chided quietly when she caught me smearing toothpaste on my visiting grandfather's neatly folded trousers. 'You have too many personalities,' she would often sigh when I lurched between tears and laughter in less than sixty seconds. Sometimes I would lure her over to the excitement of the dark side. She watched in horrified awe as I offered a babysitter 'apple juice', handing over a steaming glass of freshly decanted urine, and giggled as I placed a Whoopee cushion underneath the chair of a visiting BBC producer. But mainly our bond was rooted in the sibling language known only to us, and the secrets of our unconventional world.

Rach and I shared a room, partitioned down the middle. Our beds were separated by a bamboo curtain, a flimsy Gaza Strip that divided our territories, which were prone to constant border disputes. On Rach's side a nylon-caped William Shakespeare doll clutched a scroll next to a miniature Bible and a padlocked five-year diary marked PRIVAT!!! On mine were books with titles like *The Naughtiest Girl in the School*, glittery eyeshadows and pink hairbrushes, as well as a small shrine to Henry VIII, whose 'drive it like you stole it' approach to life had much in common with our own. And like Henry's courtiers, we never quite knew what was coming next.

It was impossible to predict what would cause a parental meltdown in our house. When, aged ten, I told my mum that I 'wasn't really enjoying' the piano lessons taught to us by a parasol-wielding diva, it triggered a long festival of mournful handwringing, punctuated by cries of 'Do you know how deeply those words hurt me?' But decanting wine into a Charles and Diana wedding flask to get drunk at school a few years later got me a 'you GUYS!' eye roll. Similarly, my father smiled indulgently when we stole his *Playboy* magazine from under the bed and produced it in front of guests but erupted in rage when he spotted a Jackie Collins novel in Rach's schoolbag. He declared it to be 'heroin of the mind' and suggested she 'wean herself on to cocaine instead,' presenting her with a Jeffrey Archer novel.

Rare visits from dog families filled me with fear. I prepared for them like military platoon inspections, encouraging my mother to wipe cobwebs off the cooker, styling her in more conservative 'mum' clothes and urging her to take down the youthful photo of her, naked, straddling Christine Keeler's infamous chair.

'Your house looks like a church. Do you really live in there?' friends would ask, poised for a tour, as their parents dropped me off after swimming parties. My T-shirt was invariably damp with a cocktail of chlorine and an outbreak of sweat at the prospect of them witnessing the noisy bohemia inside.

'Yep! See you tomorrow at school. Bye!' I would yell, abandoning manners for self-preservation, racing through the cobbled arch, past the manicured communal lawn that was maintained diligently by our neighbours. *You shall not pass*, I screamed internally. *You and your dog-family ways don't have the necessary clearance levels to cross into our peculiar sphere.* They were too pure, too equable to be greeted with my dad's wake up calls ('Hands off cocks, girls, feet in socks!'). They lacked the stomach to cope with my alcoholic grandmother's aggressive renditions of 'Delilah', as she offered Rach and me puffs on her cocktail cigarettes. And they simply weren't hardy enough to witness my mother asking the car thieves my dad was making a documentary about, 'Tell me, Keith, is this a BUSY time of year for you, work-wise?'

It was only fellow members of my parents' tribe – a collection of actors, writers, directors and intellectual *bon viveurs* armed with anecdotes – that I could tolerate crossing our threshold without mortal panic.

'Answer the door, darlings, will you?' my mother would cry from the kitchen on their arrival, as she gulped down white wine and stirred a bubbling casserole, cigarette ash occasionally garnishing her creation. Rach and I would welcome the guests. Theatre actors who justified their decision to accept a part in *Doctor Who* by roaring, 'Well, it's a "Who" not a Hamlet, but pays the BLOODY bills!' Celebrated writers, war correspondents, TV historians and broadsheet-newspaper columnists. My father would dazzle them with his observations about literature and culture and I would watch them nod approvingly at his eloquent monologues as he commanded the room with the perfect word and the precise insight.

Sometimes my parents would encourage Rach and me to put on a 'performance'. So we would traipse up to our room to hastily devise, write and produce a small comic play. My sister was the self-appointed director of these productions, and they were the only occasions when a note of tyranny crept into her otherwise benign disposition. 'Emmy! You're not taking it seriously!' she would chide. She approached our shows with a professionalism I found perplexing. Her attitude was that of the inmate who resolves to capitalise on their stretch by developing abs of steel. I was the one shouting obscenities at the guards after several ill-fated escapes. The 'look-at-me' gene I had inherited from my parents, and which had bypassed Rach completely, didn't extend to these impromptu performances. I lived in fear of being judged.

Occasionally, family friends would drop by with a symbol of a slightly less peripatetic lifestyle – my utterly longed-for dog. A showbiz lawyer came with a red setter named Jake; there was a photographer whose Dalmatian had been given the rather less child-friendly name of Lover. The house would be thrown into an explosion of tail-wagging, as the dog explored each room. Once, a dog returned with a pair of my father's Muhammad Ali pants (emblazoned with the promise 'I float like a butterfly, I sting like a bee') dangling from a slobbering jaw, to much adult hilarity.

Rach and I would race out to the garden with our temporary companion, drunk on power when they sprinted to us on command, giggling as they collapsed on us with devoted licks.

I would be inconsolable when our dog trysts came to an end, burying my head into their necks, whispering intense goodbyes like a mistress increasingly resistant to her role of weekend diversion. I was certain that these extraordinary creatures were the key to everything that was lacking in our life. The grown-ups would exchange amused glances at my histrionic farewells, promising future meetings, but these felt like hollow consolation prizes. I knew that our travelling troubadour environment was no place for a dog.

But these brief, illicit liaisons provided me with a fix that soon turned into a longing. 'PLEEEASE, please can we get a dog?' I would ask daily. My father laughed in a tone that said, 'Yeah, good luck with *that*.' He seemed as captivated as we were by our furry visitors at the time, temporarily jubilant and unconstrained. But his fear of being tethered to routine always outweighed any desire for joy if it came shackled with permanence.

My mother's reluctance to get a dog had more to do with their depressingly outdoorsy vibe. She refused to accept that anything of value ever happened outside OR before 10.00am. 'A dog is such a big responsibility, darling. And who is going to walk it?' she said, as if it were obvious that she had automatically been ruled out as a candidate.

One day my parents had some 'exciting news' for us. Rach and I had learned to be wary of statements beginning like this. At worst they led to long plane rides and introducing ourselves to new people on a different continent. At best they meant sitting in fringe theatres for three hours watching someone playing Coriolanus dressed in a leather jacket and camouflage trousers. So I was unprepared for the announcement that followed, as Rach and I gathered in the living room in our *Muppet Show* pyjamas.

'How would you like to have a doggy come to stay with us?'

'For how long?' I asked, with glass-half-empty distrust.

'A whole week.'

We could work with this.

The dog was beautiful, kind, copper-haired and called Rusty, Dad told us. Not realising he had us at 'dog'.

Rusty's 'parents' were our family friends, Joan Bakewell and her husband, Jack. The plan was that they would drop Rusty off with his basket and some belongings (he had actual belongings – how adorable!) and return the following Sunday to collect him.

In the days before Rusty's arrival I went into manic dogzilla preparation-mode, selecting towels from the airing cupboard that he might like ('Darling, that's Italian and it's from Harrods, put it back,') planning outfits that gave the impression of confident dog-family child and suggesting a trip to our butchers for treats. ('We still owe them money for those sirloins, so no, Emmy.')

Rach and I fought angrily over whose side of the room he would sleep on, before we were told that Rusty, heartbreakingly, wasn't going to be resident in either dominion. It was an unexpected show of bedroom propriety, given that Rach had recently found an abandoned bra in her bed. My mother had explained that it belonged to a friend of hers who was conducting an affair with her French lover beneath Rach's Peter Rabbit duvet. Rusty was to be allowed no such privileges. He would be installed in his basket in the living room. I imagined she was afraid he might belong to the tribe we loathed most – 'those dreadful "morning people".'

The momentous day arrived. Strung out and over-emotional from a cocktail of sleep deprivation and excitement, Rach and I kept watch with the agitation of Southern Belles awaiting returning soldiers. How could my father be engrossed in the newspaper? How could my mother be laughing throatily on the phone to an actress friend about a dreadful production of *As You Like It*, when Rusty was about to make his entrance into our lives?

'He's here!' cried Rach.

I smarted from not being the one to break the news. And then I saw him too, padding vigorously down the gravel path, glancing up at Jack with besotted reverence.

The doorbell echoed throughout the house and my parents' affable exchanges ('Hello there you bugger! You found us!') receded into background hum as I stood, staring with wonder at our new companion. Rusty assessed me with interest and then leapt into the hallway, allowing me to smother him in waves of psychotically intense love.

And so began Rusty's brief week with us: a transformative 'never-the-same-after-that-summer' episode in my life.

Rach and I loved rising early for the daily ritual of filling up his bowl with food. We giggled as he chased us up the stairs, and revelled in the novelty of being authority figures in his eyes. 'Rusty, that's VERY naughty!' we would say, giddy with power.

Sometimes I would lie in his basket just to listen to him sighing as he rearranged his limbs and half opened an eye before going back to sleep. I was overwhelmed with happiness. How could anyone not want permanent access to this source of joy? There was a glow of miraculous completeness in our household. Rusty was an anchor. My father was gleeful in his presence, and even my mother managed a walk to the shops with him, selecting a slightly lower pair of heels for the occasion.

Rach embraced the interruption of our normal life that Rusty represented but seemed less emotionally invested in it than me. She was apparently untroubled by the gloom that I knew would accompany its end. She stored good experiences like this away in a file marked 'Happy memories'. They were things that had been enjoyed rather than painful reminders of something that had passed. I harboured a sense of faint dread whenever anything too joyous came into my life: a boisterous party, a sunny day, a funny TV show. The looming ending of the moment of bliss always outweighed the present enjoyment.

All too soon, Black Sunday arrived. My mother consoled us with assurances that Joan would let us visit Rusty any time we liked, as Rach and I lay next to him stroking his soft ears. He jumped up ecstatically when Jack arrived to take him to his real home, and after the slight sting of betrayal, I resigned myself to some hard facts. We simply didn't have the requisite qualities to keep loyal, solid types like Rusty. We couldn't give them what they needed, we would only end up hurting them. It wasn't them, it was us. But our summer fling had opened up a world that I didn't want to leave. I couldn't help hoping my parents would suddenly see Rusty through my eyes, as the one that got away who forces you to swear that next time, you'll finally put a ring on it.

As autumn arrived and ushered in the excitement of our

second Christmas in Holly Village, I sensed conspiratorial anticipation in the air. My parents were exchanging knowing looks,
there were hushed phone calls and the gleeful mention of a 'big
surprise!' I didn't have to wonder what it was. I just knew.

Even they couldn't screw this up.

Chapter Two

The 'who could be at the door?' conceit was often rolled out by dog families for childhood surprises. But it had a slightly less benign sense of anticipation for Rach and me than for most ten- and eight-year-olds. We were pretty much on permanent door duty, especially if A. it was any time before 10.00am, B. there was a man carrying a briefcase and waving brown envelopes, or C. it was someone who had appeared a bit on TV in the Sixties but now stank of wine.

So when I saw our fuchsia-lipsticked maternal grandmother in diamanté-trimmed Christian Dior sunglasses and jaunty trilby standing there on Christmas Eve, my heart soared. She was holding a pet basket trimmed with a satin bow.

'SURPRISE!' she cried, with the studied enunciation of someone who probably should have left it at the third gin and tonic.

She had been tasked, a bit weirdly in retrospect, with the role of temporary guardian to our Christmas present, which I could hear scratching at the basket. Curled up inside were two creatures that would have been the stand-out choice to grace the cover of a pet magazine. But it wasn't *Puppy World* we had been presented with – it was *Cute Kittens Monthly*.

It was an unexpected twist that made a curious kind of sense. My parents had flirted with cat ownership before. Various Siamese and Burmese had all nobly shrugged off our customary 'you deserve better' speech, before we resumed our travels. Perhaps this experience had reassured my father that cats, with their beguiling but ultimately self-sufficient natures, posed no grave threat to our lifestyle.

I felt that brief stab of disappointment that comes when people offer pudding and return with a bowl of slightly tired fruit. But the sense of being swindled disappeared the moment the kittens opened their tiny mouths to meow, and thrust their little noses at the bars. They were two heavenly brown Burmese kittens – and they were all ours.

There were cries of joy as I seized the darker, more hyperactive kitten and Rach claimed the smaller, more compliant one. She examined its sleepy green eyes and soft pecan-coloured coat before pausing to ask, 'Do we get to keep them?' A pretty reasonable question considering our track record with long-term commitments.

I was enchanted by their pink scratchy tongues, neat miniature fangs and flailing paws. To me they were like a tantalising gateway drug on the way to the real stuff: a dog. 'We've got two cats,' the conversational opener could go, 'what difference will one little puppy make to our lives?'

'Can they stay in our beds tonight?' I asked. 'We promise we'll go to sleep.'

It was a pledge we had no hope of honouring without the help of prescription drugs. We stayed up most of the night, marvelling at our new playthings while the Christmas traditions played out downstairs. My grandmother was singing along to Liza Minnelli as she emptied the drinks cabinet, my mother was shrieking about 'wrapping the FUCKING Christmas presents' and my father was escaping into some light reading with *The Origin of Consciousness in the Breakdown of the Bicameral Mind*.

So it was with the joyful exhaustion of sleep-deprived new parents that Rach and I crept down the stairs on Christmas Day 1978 with our velvety new charges, to begin life as pet owners.

My father encouraged us to choose names from TS Eliot's *Old Possum's Book of Practical Cats*, in a bid to give this domestic intimacy a literary foothold. Significantly, perhaps, we were drawn to Mungojerry and Rumpleteaser, the ones described by Eliot as two glamorous, show-stopping drifters of no fixed address, who spent their lives roaming.

Tell me about it, TS.

Rach, with her gentle agreeability, stuck with the paternally approved Rumpleteaser for her kitten but I rebranded mine, deciding to trade Mungojerry for the less ornate Treacle.

After only a few seasons, Rumpleteaser suffered the fate of an actor written out of his storyline: missing, presumed 'run over'. My father, honest to the point of indecency over certain things ('Is Jim'll Fix It nice, Dad?' 'No, I'm afraid he's widely considered to be a paedophile'), was strangely coy over this disappearance. Rumple had gone on an adventure and he would turn up again, he reassured us. As time passed, though,

Rumple's mini-break was turning into a full-on Lord Lucan-style mystery.

I wasn't really prepared for the fact that pet ownership could turn out to be temporary. How could something that nuzzled up in your bed and shared your life just not be there from one day to the next? And how could everyone continue with their lives regardless?

Rach dealt with it stoically, though I did find a nod to her unprocessed grief in our battered Liberty-print address book.

'The book' was the gateway to my parents' social life. Its spine had been resealed countless times with now-yellowing Sellotape and was groaning with names scratched in by my mother in her self-taught calligraphic script. Flipping through one day past the M's – Jonathan Miller, Norman Mailer, Spike Milligan – I eventually got to the R's. And there, between the phone number for RADA and a Royal Shakespeare Company voice coach, my sister had written poignantly in blunt pencil: 'NAME: Rumple. ADDRESS: He's lost?'

My parents decided to audition a new hopeful. Kipper was already on shaky ground due to his slightly route-one birth name, and sure enough we were soon informed that he was 'just not the right fit for us, girls.' He had neither the 'look-at-me-gene' nor the devotion of a good audience, so he was sent to live with our dry cleaner, a man who paid us weekly visits and tolerated invoices being settled with coins from Rach's piggy bank. Kipper learned the hard way that cowering in the corner, recoiling at a booming actor's voice and wincing at cigarette smoke weren't going to get you far in this family.

And then another hopeful set foot on our stage. Danny. This

Burmese was the ideal male by which you judge all others – exquisite-looking, sensitive, the first to leap up to lick your tears, playful without being a nuisance, nurturing without being needy. He threatened to eclipse Treacle, but, like Rach and me, the two of them defied the odds to form a united bond. 'To be honest I'm quite relieved to have you on board, mate,' Treacle's opening gambit probably went, over dinner party leftovers. 'Don't get me wrong, they're a good laugh here. But the hours they keep take the absolute piss.'

A year after Danny's arrival, my parents called us into the living room for a chat. Rach and I had just returned from a sleepover with some dog-family school friends. There was an eerie tranquillity at home.

My father was chosen as the spokesperson for the 'very BIG' news. 'So, girls, the news . . .' he said, picking at non-existent fluff on his sleeve, 'the news is,' he repeated, like a presenter building audience tension with playful misdirection, 'that Danny . . . Danny is a DEAD pussy!'

'Danny . . . died?' Rach's voice collapsed.

'Yeeees, that's right, girls. He's a deaaad pussy!' said Dad, wrapping the whole 'death thing' in a blanket of cuteness by adopting that high-pitched tone people use when talking to a baby or suggesting a walk to a dog.

'Danny had to be put down, because . . . he had terminal CANCER!'

He gave the word 'cancer' the oddly sing-song tone of a TV prize reveal. *'You've won a holiday in MALTA!'*

Danny's death was our President Kennedy moment – incontrovertible proof that life was senseless and cruel and, in Danny's case, horribly short. We sat there, snot dribbling, tears plopping on to our T-shirts. Danny had shone so dazzlingly. It seemed impossible for him to have disappeared overnight.

'I'm going to bed!' I cried in furious protest, and Rach dutifully followed me, throwing her vote over to my rebel alliance, instead of sticking with my parents' Galactic Empire.

We lay curled up together on her duvet and Treacle licked up our cocktail of tears as he purred with slightly disrespectful bliss. This was Rach's moment as central mourner, but as always, our experience blended together to form a united one. Her losses were my losses; her bewilderment was mine. Underscoring it all was the inconvenient truth that cat ownership and Rach didn't seem to be a match made in heaven. To lose one cat may be regarded as a misfortune. To lose three? That needs a whole new word for carelessness.

'We can share Treacle if you like,' I offered as a consolation prize, aware that it was probably time to knock the endless auditions on the head. Danny's were Freddie Mercury-shoes: simply too flamboyant too fill.

But Danny's new status as 'a dead pussy' allowed Treacle to really find his light. His unique selling point for my parents lay in his good looks and fabulously laid-back approach to life. He was what my mother called 'a trooper'. Even a car accident requiring a wired jaw didn't put him out of action for long. Like us, Treacle just got on with the show. He also had a sixth sense for knowing who to cultivate, helpfully curling up in the lap of our creepy old bank manager, whom my mother would greet with tinkling laughter, hair fresh from rollers, treating us to weary side eyes as she re-filled his glass. Treacle had instinctively grasped what Rach and I had spent several years trying and failing to adjust to – the sense that we were less a family, more a touring cast of characters. Family, according to my father, was 'blind loyalty to people whose genes you happen to share': a twee, parochial concept.

People often say that when you have children you cease to be the picture; you recede into the background until you eventually become the frame. But my parents always remained the fabulously bold Jackson Pollock at the heart of our existence, with Rach and me as striking, unplanned daubs of paint on their canvas.

Even as a child, I realised that my father's desire for solitude and lack of interest in routine weren't qualities that combined easily with family life. He was brought up in material comfort, the descendant of a wealthy New Zealand timber tycoon. This meant that Rach and I had been left money in trust by a wealthy great-aunt, most of which was siphoned off for 'childhood expenses' – (the usual kind like Harrods' after-dinner mints, tax bills and Chablis). We would get updates about well-heeled cousins going to medical school and military college, conscious that we were viewed as the wayward curiosities, adding a sprinkle of glamour to their quiet, comfortable realm.

My father's privileged start in life meant he lacked the dogged ambition he observed in his friends, with their scholarships and hard-won firsts from Oxford. He preferred to bounce through life on eloquence and old-fashioned flattery. He would have once been the beating heart of a nineteenth-century literary salon, or a favoured court member at the Palace of Versailles: a cultural asset due to his intellect, wit and colossal knowledge. But his low tolerance for what he called 'flabby minds' often saw him wandering into civilian life with the heavy weaponry of the intellectual combat ring. Drinks with our neighbours would be cut short after a political argument with a dentist whose views he called 'sonorous clichés that fall like tropical rain'. He once loudly described the paintings on someone's walls as 'the sort of bland and bloodless canvasses one sees propped up against a Hyde Park railing.'

Rach and I collected these incidents, to taunt him. We would follow him around at parties, noting the remarks in a Hello Kitty notebook. We had also taken to documenting his honeyed words to attractive women, which were listed under the heading 'DAD'S CHATTER UPS!!' 'You are so beautiful, my heart threatened to leap out of its ribcage,' he said to one friend's wife. My mother simply giggled at these flirtatious moves. 'Another one for your book, girls!' she would say, enjoying the female collusion, like an elder sister indulging the clumsy romantic escapades of a brother.

That was how my mother dealt with potentially threatening moments – by turning them into entertaining anecdotes. Even her absurdly peripatetic childhood, which Dickens would have rejected as too poignantly hard-luck to get past a second draft, was served up in dinner-party-friendly morsels. She had lurched from one extraordinary adventure to another, bouncing from her native Wales to Turkey and the Sudan as my grandmother followed the next husband or lover, and then back again to England where she was shunted between friends, eventually living on her own at fifteen. It was a chaos she'd tried to escape by pushing my father into settling down, only to find herself thrust into a world of different but equally complex challenges.

The immaculate manners and superb social skills she'd acquired allowed her to infiltrate the middle classes so convincingly that no one really had any idea of the world she'd left behind. She glossed over her working-class origins and her history, immersing herself in cookery books to become literate in the French Provençal cuisine my father's friends served, and ploughing diligently through the literary tomes discussed at our salons.

But there was a high tax payable on entering this world – the sacrifice of her longing for suburban calm, to love and be loved. I sensed it when the other mums moaned about pregnancy and she reflected wistfully, ' I didn't want it to ever end!' I saw it when she calmed somebody's crying baby in five seconds flat, when she swooped in to console sad children, necklaces clinking, arms outstretched with hugs and affirmations. I felt it when we were sick and she stayed up to stroke our heads long into the night. All Daytime Mum ever wanted was that life. But Nighttime Mum had other ideas. She was the free-spirited maverick who simply couldn't plan her life around being at the school gates at a certain time; the rebellious consequence-dodger who ran up huge bills at Harrods food hall; the decadent enabler who loaned out our beds to people conducting extra-marital affairs.

I have never forgotten her telling me one day in Holly Village that all she had ever wanted was to sit at the head of a huge pine kitchen table with 'lots of children running around, and plates of lasagne and music and love.' She looked sad when she said it. It didn't sound to me then especially like the life she'd ended up with. She was less a matriarch, more a stage manager, trying desperately to control a troupe of constantly roving players.

I wonder now whether that longing for kinship was what drew her to the world of the theatres where she understudied. It was a role that played to her greatest strengths: boosting everyone's egos, providing laughter and bonhomie. They were the same qualities she brought to our own band of four when she directed our ambience, averted crises and ensured we all stuck to the comforting script of our parts. My mother was the convivial show runner, my father the indulged and unreliable star turn and I was the noisy cameo, always fighting for more stage time.

Rach's designated role was that of unconditionally adored, graceful heroine. As our family journeyed through gasoline alley throwing lit matches, she walked behind, smothering each blaze before it spread out of control. Rach was the player whose unassuming presence can make you forget their fundamental importance to the team's survival. There was a twist to the adoration we all felt for her, though. She was simultaneously up on a pedestal but perceived to be fragile, at risk of under-appreciation. If I got a good school report or a compliment there was often a whispered suggestion that we 'play it down'.

It was an issue that rose up awkwardly when my mother enrolled us in a local children's drama school called Anna Scher's. Before long I began to be offered TV work. My mother started to panic about how to sell it to Rach. 'Say it's because you're small and can play young,' she suggested when I was offered a part in a BBC adaptation of *Day of the Triffids*. 'Tell her they needed a brunette,' she whispered when I got cast in detective drama *The Professionals*.

After a while the offers of work began to fall through at the last minute. A role as Meryl Streep's daughter in the movie *The French Lieutenant's Woman* and a lead in *Swallows and Amazons* never materialised. My mother told me it was the 'up and down nature of the business'. It was only years later, when we were adults, that Rach confessed that my mother had turned the parts down. 'It was this weird thing we all kept from you. Like I gave a shit anyway,' she said.

I asked my mother about it after Rach's confession. She told me she was worried about me becoming spoilt ('At least I would have been rich and spoilt,' I sighed to my friends.) It took me a long time to consider whether it might have been tough for her to finally get that longed-for agent phone call and hear the words, 'Can I speak to the eight-year-old, please?'

In hindsight, the incident feels like a neat illustration of our family dynamic: Rach as adored but vulnerable, me as disruptive threat to the natural order. It also reflected the slightly preferential status I felt had been awarded to Rach, her sitting up front in a roomy Business Class seat while I shouted to be thrown a friggin' bone back in Economy.

As this awareness first dawned on me, during those years in Holly Village, I began to form a close bond with my father.

I asked if I could visit him at his BBC office after school, hoping to infiltrate his world and establish firm rights in his domain. My first ambassadorial visit took place when I was about nine. I carefully selected my outfit the night before – smart tasselled loafers, pink purse slung over my shoulder, vanilla lip balm to imitate the polished sheen of his glamorous female colleagues.

Once my mother had left he introduced me to a producer

called Anita. She had a glossy blonde bob and soft pastel jumper. She looked like those mums you saw on TV adverts who held up kitchen towels next to gleaming hobs. Anita congratulated me on a poem I had written about the Great Plague. 'Your dad was so proud – it was wonderful!' she said. I could work with Anita.

We surfed the corridors, the three of us, as I watched my father return respectful nods from newsreaders and presenters like a heavy-weight champion high fiving en route to the ring. His florid language and low tolerance for the basic tasks of everyday life didn't seem curious here. Everyone thought he was great.

I sat at his typewriter bashing out a letter on BBC notepaper. 'Dear Rach, I am at Dad's office, it is FUN!' It was a cruel tactic, like the *Bullseye* presenter telling contestants, 'Look what you could have won.'

My dad had his feet up on his desk and was making a phone call. 'Hello you old swine, how's the Hitler doc coming along?' Younger male producers popped in and asked his advice about documentaries, furiously making notes. He worried that TV journalism was becoming cynical and crass and often talked about 'dangerous sensationalism. You can't just pick out the eccentric fruit, you have a responsibility to describe the entire orchard.' Anita deferred softly as the men's voices got more animated, and ambitious colleagues plundered his brain for the better word or the game-changing editorial choice. This was his kingdom, and here, sitting alongside him, I realised we could exist in contentment, without reminders of the estate-car-driving dog families.

I loved resting my head on my father's shoulder as we watched

TV in Holly Village, interrogating him about movie stars he had once interviewed. He often told me about Grace Kelly, whom he called 'the melancholy princess.' 'What she gave up,' he would say, 'was, in the end, too great a sacrifice for what she gained.' He delivered this line with the impressive solemnity of a voiceover, refashioning all the Disney princess movies I had ever seen into cautionary tales about anti-feminist life choices.

The fact that my mother was dutifully preparing gammon steak the way he liked it in the kitchen, and had just agreed to change her vote in the general election to suit his beliefs, was an inconvenient truth we both decided to gloss over.

The allegiance I formed with my father could never really compete with my loyalty to the true Northern Star of my life. It was always my sister who governed my universe. She was my safe touchstone, my docking point, the lighthouse that led the way home. When I was crying, or had fallen over at school and grazed my knees, it was her name I called. 'I want Rach!' I would wail if a classmate bullied me or a teacher told me off. We fastened to each other, and forged an unshakable connection.

As we sat together on the sofa in Holly Village, watching Scooby Doo cartoons while Treacle hopped up to headbutt our chins, I increasingly felt a glow of something that had always eluded us until now – the attachment of home. But for me there was still one crucial tail-wagging element missing.

I had recently heard our plumber talking to my mum, his hand rummaging in the toilet bowl as he reflected on his marriage problems. 'I mean, if it was up to me we'd have split up. But she says we have to stay together because of the Alsatian.'

My parents found this slightly questionable logic hilarious

and 'because of the Alsatian' swiftly entered our family lexicon to refer to absurdly unconvincing excuses. But secretly, I didn't think it was ridiculous at all. Dogs were non-negotiable glue, the full stop on a life that announced to the world: 'We are normal, nothing to see here.' You couldn't just get on a plane without warning if you had a dog, leaving behind debts. Dogs forced you to stay.

Chapter Three

I was nine years old when I experienced the ache of first love. But our relationship was complicated – it always is when you fall for somebody who is Kennel Club-registered.

Ralph was the golden-haired, exuberant but well-mannered dog of my fantasies. Well-adjusted, entirely lacking in issues, he read rooms shrewdly enough to give you space but expressed infinite gratitude the minute you rattled his lead or suggested cuddle time. He even had the manners to greet guests with a classy, child-appropriate tail wag rather than an awkwardly x-rated genital examination. He smelt of grassy comfort and possessed that quality always attributed to charismatic leaders, of making you feel like the most important person in the room. But he didn't belong to me. He belonged to Lucy Simpson, the poster girl for the way the others lived. She was in my class at primary school, and I wanted her life.

Lucy wore candy-coloured espadrilles picked up on the annual family holiday to Greece and was always sitting in class, sharpened pencil poised, as I raced in with excuses about flat tyres.

At home in the evenings she gently tucked her chair into her desk after completing her spelling exercises before reading an Enid Blyton chapter and then responsibly turning out her lamp. She had her hair trimmed in a practical cut by a friendly local barber rather than a creative visionary at Vidal Sassoon who hissed, 'Oh God, *the children*,' on your entrance.

I would wistfully compare her sensible playground outfits with our clothing, the kind worn by junior Royals on balcony waves. Lucy's cords with ghostly hemlines reflected the money-conscious strategies of the dog families. My patent shoes and gold-buttoned coats were bought from a shop called Rowe's of Bond Street, who often sent us stern letters about dishonoured cheques. 'But JFK Jr wore a Rowe's coat at his father's funeral!' my mother reasoned, when I pleaded to wear Marks & Spencer like Lucy Simpson.

Lucy was the dazzling model pupil at our local school, which nestled between the blue-plaque houses of AE Housman and Charles Dickens. The school had a slightly unorthodox drama teacher who cast us as the singing corpses of sailors in a production of the *Rime of the Ancient Mariner*. 'I SHOT dead the bloody albatross!' 'They say I hanged my MOTHER!' we sang falteringly, above discordant violins.

But it was the next show, in which we had roles as radiation-stricken nuclear holocaust survivors, that saw the dog-family parents shuffling out in horror. My father dismissed their response as 'provincial squeamishness', a missile he often lobbed at people who owned a lawnmower. 'Wonderfully experimental,' my mother agreed.

The Simpsons wouldn't have called a play about a nuclear

holocaust 'wonderfully experimental'. The Simpsons had an estate car. But most of all they had Ralph, who leapt up with Pavlovian reliability to the bay window of their Edwardian semi every day to greet their bank manager father. They had a freezer stacked with Tupperware boxes, and a copy of the *Radio Times* laid neatly on the coffee table with a red ring drawn around *The Lion, The Witch and the Wardrobe*. The Simpsons had their lights on timer switches when they went on holiday because 'my dad believes in "better safe than sorry",' Lucy informed me one day as we ascended the beige-carpeted stairs to do something called 'homework'. Better safe than sorry. To me, Mr Simpson's gloriously profound maxim had more life-changing power than Martin Luther King's, 'The time is always right to do what is right.'

Lucy Simpson was the heroic ring bearer to my covetous Gollum. I sat in my dark lair yearning for the estate car her parents drove and Ralph's lead hanging on the kitchen hook: my very own 'precious' symbols. She accepted our friendship with an uncomplicated cheeriness, happy to be entertained by my noisy stories and flattered by my desire to infiltrate her domestic realm. She shook her head good-naturedly at my extrovert displays, using parentally friendly rebukes like 'bloody bonkers!' and 'that's a bit crackers!'

Mr Simpson sent postcards when he went away on business trips. They were propped up neatly on the mantelpiece and stuck to a standard theme. 'Lovely food. Missing you!' From the front they looked no different to the ones my father occasionally sent from his documentary-making trips. A hulking Edinburgh Castle or an Eiffel Tower. But when you turned my father's over, things deviated slightly from Mr Simpson's script.

Dear Em and Rach,
Venice is all your dreams of gracious living in
blindingly lovely circumstances come suddenly true.
But what a dark history of plague and blood-stained
suffering between all the good bits. I guess that's
the price you pay for defying the gods of modesty and
logic by building this metropolitan masterpiece on a
god-forsaken marsh. If so, it was worth every lira.
All love, Dad

Occasionally the worlds of the opposing postcards collided when we hung out with the Simpsons *en famille*. I took these visits as my chance to clarify to my parents the goals they should be working towards, like a life coach using envy as a motivating principle. But my family was a tough crowd, baffled by my obsession with this organised household. Rach was unimpressed by their shiny kitchen gadgets, my father examined their book-shelves critically and my mother always requested an ashtray on arrival and encouraged them to open more wine, polluting their pristine atmosphere with our signature decadence.

A sense of unease descended upon me during these visits. I feared the moment when my father would start talking about capitalism, bringing his intellectual weight into friendly chatter about holidays and school fetes. My mother would elegantly swerve the conversation away from polemics, delving into her box of anecdotes and steering the chat into less perilous terrain. But it was much easier to navigate dog families like the Simpsons as a solo explorer. I learned how to shape-shift and blend in, observing the way they behaved and adopting the vernacular of the children, swapping profanities for 'absolute wally' and 'that's your hard cheddar.' I made sure I was the first one up in the mornings, to suggest that for me, an early family breakfast was the most natural thing in the world.

Even the sources of the Simpsons' infrequent conflicts seemed refreshingly uncomplicated. They disagreed about whose turn it was to be the top hat in Monopoly and whether to play Phil Collins in the car. Instead of, 'How long is that fucking Chilean concert pianist sleeping on the sofa for?' (Answer? Indefinitely.)

The Simpsons had a country cottage in Suffolk and sometimes I was invited up to experience dog-family weekends. We would pile into their dad's car, a tin of travel sweets nestling by the gearstick, and play I-Spy while Ralph slept obediently behind his dog guard. 'Who wants to go and pick samphire for tea?' asked their mum, Sally, when we arrived, discreetly swapping my patent shoes for a pair of borrowed wellies. And off we would race through the salt marshes, Ralph running ahead of us, his tail wagging excitedly. We'd play board games and go for 'drives', stopping off at country pubs to order scampi, before baths and tea and 'just one chapter of your books!' before lights out.

It seemed on those weekends with the Simpsons that I had been given a pass to an entirely different way of life, where there was a clear division between adults and children. A place where people settled disputes without soliloquies and quotes from Phillip Larkin.

Did everyone else experience these pangs of confusion when they went to stay with other families? As bags were packed for our return to London, I felt a sense of disloyalty, as if I were returning to people who were utterly blind to my emotional betrayal. Lucy and her sister Jessica would fall asleep in the car and I would stare out at the disappearing tranquillity of the countryside, stuck between fascination for this other life and the relief of returning to the familiarity of my warmly eccentric family realm.

Looking in through the Gothic-arched window at our peculiar world as Treacle rushed across the lawn to greet me, his jewelled collar glinting decadently, I felt a glow of belonging. I envied the Simpsons' life, but those people in that strange Gothic house? They were my gang. And gangs stuck together.

Chapter Four

One night, Rach and I were woken up by the sound of my mother shouting. Drama wasn't unprecedented in Holly Village but there was something about this particular altercation that felt off-brand. We rushed to position ourselves at the top of the stairs to eavesdrop. My father yelled back a bit and then a door slammed, putting an end to our stakeout as we scampered back into our bedroom for a post-mortem through the Gaza Strip.

My parents had never really indulged in epic marital rows. My mother would dismantle my father's occasional bursts of irritation with the soothing tones of the hostage negotiator. Veiled hostility and closed doors were a foreign country to us as we played out our disputes noisily *en masse*. But silence was becoming a new weapon in my mother's arsenal, the most deadly strike of all when introduced into an atmosphere of constant noise.

Something was definitely up in Holly Village.

My father had started spending all his time closeted away,

speaking softly on the phone to Anita, Mum's heel-clacking return from the theatre woke us up later than usual, and was often followed by my father descending the stairs forcefully. On the rare nights they were in together, the curious concept of something called 'bedtime' was enforced.

One Saturday afternoon Rach decided to investigate by raiding their bedroom drawers as my father snoozed in front of a Bing Crosby film. My mother had gone off for lunch with her gay theatre friends at a members' club called Zanzibar.

As Rach performed a hurried Watergate sweep of the drawers, I kept lookout, like the slightly dozy member of the gang who can't be trusted with anything more technical.

'Look, I found his diary!' she hissed triumphantly. 'It's mostly stuff about books,' she continued with disappointment, flicking through the pages. 'What's "conjugal rights"?'

I shrugged, imagining my father performing some ritual involving animal sacrifices around a bonfire.

This kind of sly investigation was one we hadn't been reduced to before in our egalitarian troupe. We knew everything about their relationship – the letter Mum had found from another woman in the early days of their courtship. The married man my mum had a secret crush on. The reason my dad's first marriage to a woman called Shirley had failed. ('I got swept up in the expectations of others.') And now this weird line was being drawn between us and adult matters. The idea of my parents having an interior life that didn't include us seemed preposterous.

My mother started shipping us off to our grandmother's flat every weekend. She insisted this was so that we could have 'quality time with your grandmother', but there was a non-negotiable sense of urgency about the trips. It felt as if a vital page had been ripped out from our story.

'Why do we have to spend every weekend with Nan?' Rach moaned one day as we transferred our duvets and pillows into the car. 'She's always drunk!'

'And she takes us to a pub where Rastafarian men offer us RUM,' I added self-righteously.

And so, one Friday, weighed down wearily like Atlas with our duvets, we rang the intercom of the Brixton flat. Ready to spend the long weekend with our fabulously entertaining but alcohol-fond grandmother. We ascended the staircase that smelt of ammonia and said hello to Lou – a homeless prostitute my grandmother had effectively sublet the stairwell to, who smiled hazily at us through her toothless grin.

My grandmother's cats were scuttling about inside the flat. Lucky was black with white tuxedo markings and greeted visitors like a rural pub regular discovering a tourist in his seat. My grandmother cited 'shyness' to excuse his basic lack of people skills. Simon was his panicked sidekick, a tortoiseshell with a blotchy ochre coat who had obvious co-dependency issues. They were less domestic pets, more two pairs of terrified glassy eyes and eight scuttling legs, who spent their days glowering behind sofas. They emerged only to attack a bowl of Whiskas or pee on a coat before returning to the shadows.

'What is the POINT in having bloody cats if they're going to behave like these ones?' my mother always said when she dropped us off, appalled by their stage fright.

Rach and I usually ended up abandoning our attempts to

draw Lucky and Simon out from a corner. My grandmother would imply that once we had all left, liberated from our judgmental presence, they would transform into clever, charismatic extroverts. Simon, she claimed, had even mastered the art of saying 'mama'. It was like someone telling you their dour, standoffish friend is 'just hilarious!' when you get to know them.

Perhaps Lucky and Simon were suffering from severe post-traumatic stress disorder. They'd been sold life with a pensioner and ended up with a woman who saw off a burglar by pulling down his trousers, sending him fleeing as he screamed, 'BITCH!'

If my parents were the ringmasters at the circus of our childhood, my grandmother was the bearded lady – exotic, extraordinary, almost the stuff of legend. She wasn't much like my school friends' grandmothers, who had Murray Mints and tissues stored in their cardigan pockets. They hadn't made their way through five husbands, had a secret child with an American colonel and dated a Turkish man who called himself 'the king's messenger'. Those nanas tended not to go by several different names, either. Josie, Ivy-May and Lingy-Loo were three that Rach and I used for her, depending on the situation.

Even now I hardly know what to say when people ask about her life. Which one? Cabaret dancer in Wales or governess in Turkey for the American colonel who'd secretly fathered her son? The woman who illegally started a school in Nigeria or the one who helped the southern rebels during the Sudanese civil war? Her romantic encounters took her around the globe, followed by my bewildered mother, who escaped to London at fifteen to go to drama school. Plane tickets would arrive occasionally for her to join my grandmother on the latest leg of her world tour.

Nan was now settled in a crumbling Victorian mansion flat behind Brixton tube station, back when the area was a locale entered with trepidation by reporters covering the 1981 riots. This unfortunate detail wasn't about to let my parents keep us from our suddenly vital 'quality time' with our grandmother, though. If the news bulletins reflected an especially bad night of rioting, my father would take charge of driving duties, dodging hurled bottles and police lines, to ensure our safe delivery.

My grandmother was one of those women whose name was always mentioned with the supporting caveat of 'a great beauty in her day'. There was an antique dressing table where she sat every morning, layering her face in creamy powder, feathery eyelashes and magenta lipstick. She sipped tea from her chipped china cup, cigarette burning out in the matching saucer, while Eighties breakfast shows blasted from her portable TV. She had grown up in an era when personal traumas were dealt with by adopting the maxim 'Pour yourself a drink, put on some lipstick and pull yourself together.' Especially, in her case, the 'pour yourself a drink' part.

'Christine, tell us about your bizarre mother!' my mum's friends would cry, intrigued by this strange female who had abandoned all the beats of convention.

My mother dutifully trotted out the wild stories about my grandmother – how she'd used beauty and charisma as currency to escape her almost feral childhood in Wales and become a jet-setting femme fatale. How her men were like expendable members of a relay team: the starter husband in Wales relinquishing the baton to the painter who took her to Africa, who passed it to a colonial type, who handed it to a handsome Nigerian, over to a man simply known as Joe. Before it was restored to the starter husband once again. And all of them seemed happy to ignore the endless pit stops on the way for her endless lovers.

The hordes of men my grandmother got through were part of her story but she was the one driving the narrative. That shift that women entering middle age are expected to make, from centre-stage coquette to hazy backdrop, was one she refused to acknowledge. Her sense of entitlement was never slung out along with her youthful beauty. If anything it became an even more ferocious blaze.

As we entered Nan's flat the cats scuttled away on cue. Her lodger sat on the sofa, eating beans and chips. He was a quiet, timid man from Hull who most of the time would pad unobtrusively around her flat, blushing at her bawdy manner. But she had spent the last few months giving him a makeover. He had a new name – 'Johnny da Silver' – and a new career. As a stripper. 'I've given him SUCH confidence, girls!' she would cry, kissing her fingertips like an Italian chef camping it up on daytime TV.

But the reviews weren't needed – we had seen Johnny da Silver in full flow ourselves. Rather considerately he abridged his strip for us. Perhaps he felt that a ten- and twelve-year-old might not be the right demographic for his final reveal.

'Lovely little mover!' my grandmother cried, clapping, as the bottle of Gordon's was slowly depleted.

I would wonder at these moments how the Simpsons were spending their weekends. Watching *Flash Gordon* at the cinema? Playing Ludo as they drank orange squash?

Tonight we were spared the free show. At around midnight, woozy from the sips of Babycham Nan gave us as a 'little treat' to go with our illicit cigarettes, Rach and I headed into my grandmother's bedroom to try to get some sleep. Before it all kicked off.

The Lambeth town-hall clock was striking 2.00am when my grandmother banged on the light switch and burst into the bedroom. She wore a silk turban, silent-movie-star make-up and the ominous stare of the combative drinker. She was carrying a plastic portable cassette recorder that was blasting out Turkish folk music. 'Where is LOVE?' she bellowed belligerently.

'Nan! Piss off, you're drunk!' Rach shouted, disappearing under the duvet.

'Listen you me well!' she continued, deploying the Nigerian pidgin she favoured whenever she was drinking. 'Where is LOVE? Where is LOVE in this 1981?'

It was quite a question to have to answer at 2.00am. But luckily she was on hand to do that for us.

'Let me tell YOU. Let me TELL YOU. BABY.'

The 'baby' was spat out contemptuously. She paused and exhaled with theatrical exhaustion, as if she were anticipating applause.

'There IS no LOVE in this 1981. How's about THAT. BABY!' Then, her eyes glittering dangerously, she slammed the door and Simon and Lucky scuttled off like terrified witch's familiars.

Rach and I dissolved into exhausted giggling fits. We were, as ever, slightly high on the thrill of witnessing an adult lose their composure so comprehensively.

She returned for an encore, thrusting black and white photographs at us, roaring, 'I remember when my daddy was shot DEAD! They shot him DEAD, BABY!' It was an unusual way of revealing distressing information about a deceased relative. Not the way I've seen it done on *Who Do You Think You Are?*

Some nights she would get out photos of our five grandfathers. Bayo, our Nigerian grandfather (number four or was it five? It was hard to keep track), had been around during our early childhood. He spoke in curious English, influenced by old newsreels. 'I like the gracious Queen, TOO much,' he would say. My parents often told dinner-party stories about Bayo to make their friends laugh, recalling the time he had marched my grandmother up to the police station to report her for 'wifely disobedience'.

One day we had heard them use a curious word to describe him.

'What does bigamist mean, Dad?' Rach asked.

That marked the end of that particular grandfather.

Nan had decided to live out her old age alone, although the Welsh starter husband (our actual grandfather) came to visit occasionally. My mum referred to him as 'my mother's first husband', perhaps preferring not to access any sense of paternal abandonment she felt.

In public my mother laughed about my grandmother's chaotic life but when she spoke of her in private, Mum's voice always took on a slightly different tone. She would sigh and say things about us not 'knowing the half of it'. But when I watched my mother in her incarnation as Nighttime Mum, I was reminded sometimes of that wild spirit and refusal to conform.

My grandmother had a daytime persona, too. Nighttime Nan was unpredictable but Daytime Nan blanketed Rach and me in bottomless devotion, massaging our feet, serving grapes in a carved African wooden bowl and sending us postcards listing our superlatives ('You are the best of the best!!'). She liked extremes. Her heart was 'ripped into a thousand pieces!' if we snapped at her, the newsagent who shortchanged her was a 'wicked, wicked soul.' It felt at times as if the weekly immersion in her life were some sort of odd joke. 'You think *you're* not like the others? Hold my beer.' But her utter bizarreness began to make our own lifestyle seem almost suburban by comparison.

Sometimes my grandmother found herself thrust into one of my parents' literary evenings. The guests would listen to her stories about Africa: the time she'd hidden Sudanese children in wardrobes during the civil war and plied soldiers with alcohol and charm, like a deviant *Sound of Music* Abbess.

At the time I worried we were betraying her by wheeling her out as the freakish turn. It wasn't until my own adulthood that I considered what it must have been like for my mother, growing up in that endless turmoil. There was so much she hadn't told us. Details would emerge of things she had witnessed, things that couldn't be incorporated into the construct we all fashioned, of my grandmother as an ebullient, vivacious character. I suspect that some of it my mother couldn't face, and some of it she had simply filed away with all the other crazy shit.

Sometimes she would drop tasters in casually, as if she were reminiscing about family trips to the seaside. I remember us watching the movie *Airplane*. When the pilot character delivered the comically surreal line, 'Joey, have you ever been inside a Turkish prison?' to a child onboard, my mother whispered, 'Well, I have, as a matter of fact.' Years later, as teenagers, we were flicking through old photo albums and came across a picture of her holding up a Sudanese baby. 'Oh, that was Abdullatief, darling. Nan adopted him from a brothel. They took him during the war. So she sort of . . . lost touch.'

They? Who were *they*? And how did my grandmother manage to 'lose touch' with a baby? Expecting the baby to send updates seemed to me a big ask.

Mum laughed at our stunned reactions to her exotic history. Her detachment perhaps only possible once she could breathe, at a safe distance from my grandmother's vast presence.

I was almost in awe of the breezy tone she used for these thunderbolts. I realised that she had happily survived an itinerant chaos that made our lives seem pastoral. But the unpredictability that she had vowed to escape had still found a way into our life. It turns out the past can be annoying like that, emerging when you least expect it to claim its rights to the story.

Returning from our weekly dips into my grandmother's tornado made me feel safe in Holly Village, where people used alcohol to ease the social flow rather than to bury trauma. Where we didn't get woken up at 2.00am to answer questions like 'where is love?' and hear about people being shot. (The Chilean concert pianist tended to avoid discussions about Pinochet.)

I might have raged against the unconventional details of our life but the captains of our ship hadn't abandoned the controls entirely.

Well, not yet.

Chapter Five

My mother had started reading the kinds of books you wouldn't find on the Simpsons' shelves. One was called *A Woman in Your Own Right – Assertiveness and You*. It joined a growing collection of similar books piled up on her bedside table. They had titles like *The Myth of the Vaginal Orgasm*, *The Women's Room* and *When I Say No, I Feel Guilty*, which posed the question 'Are YOU letting people walk all over you?' on its cover.

The books seemed to have coincided with a new dynamic in our family. My mother had acquired a distinct air of rebellion. She cultivated single friends and spent hours drinking white wine in the kitchen with a frizzy-haired divorced woman who always sighed, 'Well, that's MEN for you!' She began to respond to my dad in a different tone, saying things like, 'Actually, I enjoyed that book!' and 'I happen to like Elton John. I'll play what I want!' And sometimes she dropped in mentions of his friend Anita that didn't sound altogether friendly.

I found it all a bit exhausting.

Rach would seize *A Woman in Your Own Right* from my mother's room and scornfully read passages aloud to me. 'Listen to this! "Are you a martyr at home? How do you respond if everyone leaves the cleaning to you?"'

The book advised stating your needs in clear language and using the prefix, 'I *appreciate* you want me to do that BUT . . .'

'I *appreciate*' evolved into comedy gold for us, and our father became a co-conspirator as we hurled the phrase around. 'I *appreciate* you want me to turn the TV down . . .' we would say, in sanctimonious American accents, as he laughed in shared delight.

My mother had also started to spend a lot of time visiting our pop star neighbour, Lynsey de Paul, who had just returned from a long spell visiting her boyfriend in Los Angeles. She lived in solitary splendour in one of the most fairy-tale dwellings in our gated community. 'I bought this house myself – so no man can ever tell me what to do in it. Do you know how great that feels, girls?' she once said to us.

Rach and I observed our mother through Lynsey's windows as we sat in the garden, both of them gesticulating wildly, lost in adult female discussion. Sometimes they caught sight of us and broke off to give us slightly panicked smiles, like unsuccessful award nominees sensing a looming camera.

As I got to know Lynsey during her summer back in London, I realised I had never met anyone like her before. She certainly wasn't one of Cookie Monster's regimented plates of cookies. There was no sensible dad, Tupperware boxes or a tail-wagging Ralph at the heart of her home, but for some reason it didn't matter. Her non-conformity was presented with such forthright, glamorous entitlement you had no option but to be hopelessly enthralled by it.

Until I met Lynsey, the women I knew who lived alone were retired headmistresses and widows, not dazzling self-made goddesses who drove fast cars and used the C-word with abandon. She had a fierce tongue, terrifying temper and low tolerance for 'assholes'. She didn't tread around men in that gentle, coercive way I often witnessed.

In fact, she didn't tread around anyone. She once told my mother about a school reunion and an old classmate who had abandoned her Oxford degree to get married. 'Shame on you,' Lynsey had announced. 'Waste of a place at Oxford!'

It left me with a lingering sense of awe. It was thrilling that someone could disregard the social contract so recklessly. How could anyone be so removed from the need to be likeable? Her entire essence was a firm 'screw you' to the dog families. But, confusingly, I admired her. I had only ever seen men behaving with this level of fiery confidence – roaring around in sports cars, yelling swear words and throwing money and power at problems. I didn't know women could do that.

Aunty Lyn (as she liked us to call her) had become cele-brated for her ballads about love, narrowly missing out on first place in the Eurovision Song Contest. She had an iconic beauty spot above her lip that I saw her painting in with a brown eyeliner one day. 'It's a chicken pox scar!' She smiled. 'DON'T tell any journalists, Emmy!' As if my Paddington Bear address book was bursting with the numbers of *Daily Mail* diarists.

She had marble telephones, a glass coffee table held up by

stone Chinese lions, a framed photo of her laughing elegantly at something Prince Charles had just said and a glare that warned, 'Don't-fuck-with-me, fellas'. I remember the first time I saw her, as her 4-foot 11-inch frame floated out of her ivy-covered Gothic door, buttery blonde crimped hair falling to her waist, glinting four-inch heels hitting the gravel path with purpose, white coat sweeping behind defiantly.

'CHRISTEEENE!' she hollered at my mother, as our new friendship developed, using her set of keys to enter our house without knocking, smelling of wealth and sex appeal. She refused wine, ('No thanks, I quite like not having grey skin') reviewed our plates of ham with disgust ('Enjoying your dead animal?') and responded to my mother's apology for smoking with, 'I'd rather you crapped on the carpet but, sure, go ahead.'

Her house was geographically next to ours but it felt like the kingdom beyond the wardrobe with Lynsey as glittering snow queen. If you really were hell-bent on not living like the others, this, perhaps, was the way to go about it.

Rach and I drank Coca-Cola out of her crystal wine glasses, sitting on Gothic oak chairs, while she discussed her ex-boy-friends. They included Ringo (Starr), Dudley (Moore), Dodi (Fayed), a married screen icon and Roy Wood, the lead singer of Seventies pop group Wizard. I'd seen photos of him and he looked slightly scary, something she seized upon whenever a newspaper described her as 'a plus-one to debonair men.' 'I dated a guy with green hair, for fuck's sake!'

We were hugely flattered by Aunty Lyn's cultivation of our family. Her interest in us was partly due to relief at finding fellow oddballs in our quiet neighbourhood. But we all knew that the real deal-closer was Treacle. She would scoop him up into her glossy embrace and steal him away to lovingly paint his claws with clear polish. Sometimes I would find him gobbling up fresh salmon from an Art Deco bowl. Then eyeing me smugly as if to say, 'Bitch – this is how we do it now.'

'Where on earth is Treacle?' my mother asked one evening, and Rach and I headed out to investigate the cemetery. Until we caught a glimpse of our cat perched like an Egyptian figurine, in the seductive glow of Lynsey's living room. We were now the helpless teenage sweetheart to his just-signed footballer, watching him shift into a tempting world that lay beyond us. 'He's more like a lodger these days,' my father said, delighted that Treacle had been savvy enough to pick such a dazzling part-time mistress.

Sometimes Aunty Lyn invited us over for 'a girls sleepover!' in her Elysian turret. She sat Rach and me on a chair in her mirrored make-up room, painting our lips scarlet and our eyes gold, ringleting our hair and draping us in bespoke designer gowns. 'I wore that to Studio 54. It looks GREAT on you!' she told me. 'Princess Diana's designers made that for me!' she said to Rach.

Our friendship with Lynsey, who was the subject of much gossip in our local area, intrigued the dog families when she strode into school fetes in leather trousers and Cartier sunglasses. The philosophers with dandruff, the foreign correspondents whose spittle landed on the table when they talked about books – they weren't the most persuasive advert for our unorthodox lifestyle. But Lynsey's confident glamour cast our difference in an altogether more attractive light. Her refusal to sublimate herself into anyone else's way of thinking was intoxicating. She lived her life not as an endlessly charming guest but as the resolutely uncompromising CEO of her world.

'You remind me of me, Emmy,' she once told me as we ate spaghetti in her kitchen. 'You're strong and sparky.'

I absorbed this praise with a hint of shame because in truth, I wasn't like her at all. I was strong and sparky in her presence because I knew that was what she wanted. I was dutiful in the presence of the dog families because that was what they expected. Boisterous and precocious in front of my parents' friends because that went down well with them. Playing at being different people was all I had ever known; unlike Rach, who seemed exasperatingly committed to remaining the same person in every environment.

'I never borrow clothes,' Lynsey once said. 'Why would I want to walk into a room as someone else?' I realised this was perhaps all I had ever wanted to feel.

One of the things that made me happiest was trying on her designer dresses. Catching sight of myself in the mirror, I felt as if I had temporarily absorbed some of her magnificent power. They weren't so much clothes, more spectacular armour, with huge shoulders and sweeping sleeves. They reminded me of the women I had seen in soaps like *Dynasty* and *Dallas*, which my father watched with me. ('Well, even shit has its own integrity,' he would say, guiltily.) They were clothes for women who closed discussions by snapping, 'Waiter – cheque please!' and who told boardrooms of men 'not to underestimate me', before departing in outrage.

By the end of the summer, Lynsey's domain had become

Treacle's almost-full-time residence. He juggled our two houses with the wily charm of a playboy cultivating a harem of exes. Until one morning, Lynsey crunched up the gravel path wrapped in a Cruella de Vil coat with two impossibly handsome Burmese kittens all of her own, named Louis and Bix. Treacle responded with outright hostility, thrusting his backside in her face and retreating to lick his wounds. He slunk back into our shabby world, scarred forever from getting so close to Lynsey's blistering star.

Perhaps it was his very own 'return from the Simpsons' moment. It takes an Icarus to know one.

'He HATES Lynsey now!' Rach said. My parents laughed in agreement.

But none of us were prepared for the unlikely cat whisperer who was about to arrive.

I'd heard a lot about James Coburn, Lynsey's boyfriend in LA. I knew he was famous, best known for his starring roles in movies like *The Magnificent Seven* and *The Great Escape*. That he had won an Oscar, owned a fleet of Ferraris and that his mate 'Steve' had the surname McQueen. But I hadn't anticipated what a towering, magnetic colossus James would be in person, with his huge glittering smile, thick silvery hair and growling Darth Vader voice.

'Hey, Emmy, I'm James,' he said with a grin on our first meeting, revealing thoroughbred teeth and extending a powerful forearm to embrace me in a vast hug. It was hard to see him as a cinematic titan as he spread out lazily on the sofa in slippers, reading the Sunday papers, talking about his problems with arthritis and chuckling obediently at Lynsey's jokes. But I saw everyone behave differently around James when he entered a room. People adjusted themselves instinctively, adopting deferential body language.

Everyone, that is, except Lynsey.

'James, come on, help me with the bins!' she would cry as he lumbered up from the sofa, adjusting his kimono to avoid a reveal. I flinched when she addressed him with such casual bossiness. She spoke to him as if he were a normal man. Which seemed a terrible idea.

After one trip to LA, he and Lynsey returned with gold 'E' and 'R' necklaces for us, each with a sparkling diamond at the centre. 'Don't write "James Coburn got me a diamond necklace" in your school holidays project, darling,' my mother advised. 'It sounds a bit *showy*.' But the diamond necklace wasn't what sold me on James. It was his extraordinary self-possession.

My grandfather visited us that summer from his sleepy beach town in New Zealand. He was a sweetly gentle, slightly deaf and hopelessly absent-minded GP. He wore a beret, regularly left stool samples in the boot of his car and liked to quote Tolstoy at his bemused patients. So James Coburn's cinematic dominance was lost on him.

'What was your name, Cockburn you say?' he asked James.

I looked to Rach with horror.

Rach suppressed a giggle, as she tended to in situations like this. *So what, Em?* her look said. *Why do you care so much?*

Why don't YOU? said my hostile return glance.

'Coburn, Sir, it's Coburn,' James replied, with the respectful tones of someone who has served military duty addressing an elder.

When my mother and Lynsey were closeted away in her kitchen having one of their long chats, James would be charged with the role of babysitter. 'James! Play Boggle with the girls,' Lynsey instructed him one afternoon as we sat in her garden. She clacked around in slingbacks and obscene cut-off denims, fetching us orange juice before retreating to the kitchen and their private discussions.

Clad in his black silk dressing gown, James placed his huge tanned hands on the miniature egg timer and thrust it upside down before gently prompting us with word suggestions. 'Fad? Great choice, Rach!' he boomed encouragingly. He puffed on his cigar, his large frame almost overwhelming Lynsey's tiny garden chairs, coaxing Treacle towards him with the self-confident charm of the never-knocked-back.

Treacle had been observing James's presence from the safety of the bushes for several weeks. One day he emerged cautiously, trying to decide whether his curiosity outweighed his hurt pride. 'Hey Treac!' James whispered, holding out tapered fingers. 'Come on Treac, come on Treac, baby.' After several weeks of this encouragement, Treacle swallowed his shame and settled contentedly in James's lap. His return to Arcadia was complete. Like the rest of us, Treac baby was powerless to resist Uncle James's magnetic signal.

It felt odd seeing Lynsey suddenly sharing the space she loudly dominated, especially with someone who commanded rooms without uttering a word. The high-status men we knew tended not to have look-at-me partners like Lynsey. This was a domestic realm I hadn't seen before, one governed by two equally powerful emperors.

Sometimes they would take Rach and me to the shops, Lynsey marching ahead in her heels, James strolling along, spotted silk hanky poking out of his linen blazer, black shades protecting him from the perpetual gaze of the world. They stood out, with their conscious entitlement, architects of their exotic difference. 'We're not like you, so we're not going to even try to be like you.'

One day Lynsey decided that Treacle 'urgently' needed the vet, as she often did (a broken claw was enough), so Rach and I clambered into her Jaguar as James arranged his limbs awkwardly and dutifully extinguished his cigar. He emerged with us to ring the Sellotape-covered doorbell of the vet's ramshackle practice, crouching to enter its tiny front room as pensioners with marmalade cats eyed him with shock that bordered on outrage. He seemed curiously vulnerable at those times, like Gulliver, too mountainous to really work in our little north-London world.

A few months later my mother told us that James wasn't coming back to Holly Village. Lynsey talked to us about everything having a life and a death. 'Flowers, people. And love can be like that, too.' She looked puffy-eyed, and I heard her mentioning something about 'commitment' to my mother. Her space suddenly seemed tinged with absence. My mother told us that Lynsey had escaped a difficult childhood and underneath her ferocious exterior was 'just a frightened little girl.' Which didn't really fit with my notion of her as fiery goddess whom I wanted to imitate.

Within a few weeks her waspish humour was back. She told me when I'd had a dramatic haircut, 'What do you mean "try everything once?" Try cutting off your head, see how you like *that*.' As were her collection of 'walkers': a bunch of citrus-scented male friends who took her to premieres and cocktail parties, occasionally providing a burst of overnight activities she referred to as 'medicinal'.

Some of the playground mums came over to gossip about the end of Lynsey's relationship with James. They had read about it in the papers. 'She's all alone in that big house. It's sad really,' they said, with a concern that I knew sounded phoney even if at the time I didn't know why.

It was only years later that something struck me about the end of Lynsey's love affair. She didn't seem diminished by the removal of James's unquestionable power and status. Her life remained intact. She saw the same friends, got invited to the same parties and drove the same sports car with noisy abandon. She had never changed her vote to please him, held back her opinions or taken up less space to accommodate his dominance. So she returned to a self that hadn't been reduced. People often described her as 'difficult', 'impossible' or 'frightening' – most of which was undeniably true. But perhaps that was the way she had to be, as an early female settler, hacking through the undergrowth with a machete to clear the path for other women – all those who wanted to live a life that was based on being more than an adjunct to someone else.

It was Lynsey who inadvertently introduced me to another female who was fond of doing things in a different way.

I had occasionally spotted a girl, who looked as if she too might be around eleven years old, walking up the gravel path to Lynsey's house. The girl was usually talking animatedly with her mum and always dressed in the kind of fashionably dis-arrayed outfits that pop stars wore, radiating an air that didn't belong to coastal walks and ringed viewing in the *Radio Times*. Sometimes I would peer at her through the window before leaping back, not wanting her to discover the secrets behind our Gothic portal.

But she favoured a rather more direct approach. I answered our door one day to see her standing there, in an orange fishnet top and tiny black leather jacket, smiling confidently. 'Hi, I'm Jane,' she said, 'my mum's at Lynsey's. Do you want to hang out?'

Hang out? It sounded so sophisticated and cool, the way people in American bands probably addressed each other. And suddenly, Rach and I had a new best friend called Jane Goldman.

Jane didn't eat last night's canapés for breakfast. Her house, which was only a few miles away from ours in nearby Hampstead, didn't have Chilean concert pianists sleeping on the sofa. And her bed wasn't loaned out for illicit affairs. But her parents, Stu and Mandy, laughed tolerantly when Jane called her cat Mims 'a little fucker', allowed us to play Culture Club loudly and told us we looked 'wonderful, darlings!' when we made dresses out of black bin liners and paraded down the street. They lived in a mews house with fashionable Eighties phone cables in bright colours, and had a video camera, with which we recorded a series of improvised plays. I felt safe enough in this liberal environment to pull back the curtain slowly on our own eccen-tricities, which were greeted with cries of 'that's hilarious!' rather than sidelong glances.

Jane's mother, Mandy, was also a recent convert to my mother's female empowerment bible *A Woman in Your Own Right*, and we bonded with Jane over the shared inconveniences we were experiencing as a result of this stupid book. The three of us decided the simplest way to re-educate our mothers was via a passive-aggressive sketch, which we filmed and forced them to watch.

'I APPRECIATE your child has been hit by a car but I can't take him to the hospital as I am READING MY BOOK!' we whined, in Californian accents, hoping they would see the grave consequences of their dangerous free-thinking. But Mandy and my mother just howled with laughter. I felt a sense of pride at being the architect behind our collective friendship with the Goldmans. It was a friendship thrillingly unique to Rach and me, one cultivated rather than inherited, that couldn't be threatened by adult tension over politics and loans.

Jane's mum Mandy had been friends with Lynsey long before she'd arrived in Holly Village, since they were twentysomethings. Mandy was vivacious, wore Vivienne Westwood creations and red lipstick, allowed us to swear and called everyone 'darling', all of which enabled me to see my mother's unconventional maternal energy though a more tolerant prism.

Rach and I were deeply envious of Jane's bedroom, a fantasy kingdom with a dressing table stocked with brightly hued make-up. 'I call that blusher "the killer", watch out!' she'd warn us. She had a pale pink sofa for entertaining and a coffee table covered in piles of subculture magazines like *The Face*. She played us David Bowie's *Aladdin Sane*, talked about horror movies and carried a bottle of Perrier every day as a lifestyle accessory. The pretty blonde icons my friends admired were absent from her world; the aspirational picture on her wall was of a dungaree-wearing character called Doris from the TV show *Fame*, famous for her smart remarks. Jane took a kettle as a handbag into school, and if her classmates sniggered at her it simply seemed to validate her belief that different was better.

By the time we were turning into teenagers, Jane, Rach and I had become a gang all of our own. We used to pile into Jane's mum's white Mini and she would drop us in Covent Garden, me in Jane's trilby and garish make-up, feeling like a glamorous pop star, Rach and Jane similarly decked out in odd ensembles, all of us giggling, singing and celebrating our difference rather than trying to fit in. It felt strangely liberating not to be hiding. Rach and I were no longer posing as members of a club to which we would never really belong. It was as if we had finally been offered membership to a different place: one where we were accepted. Just as we were.

Although, in retrospect, the trilby really was a colossal mistake.

Chapter Six

'It's morally wrong!' my father declared.

My parents were arguing about education. My mother had managed to charm a huge loan out of our sleazy bank manager, in order to send us both to a smart private school for our secondary education. It was one of the first times she had openly defied my father over a big life decision. I suspected it had a lot to do with *A Woman in Your Own Right*.

'He's hiding behind politics,' she told Rach and me. 'Mean bugger doesn't want to cough up!'

I had never seen her like this before, insistent and angry. She told us she needed to ensure we had a future where we weren't 'dependent on a sodding man!'

My father's refusal to involve himself in any sort of life admin eventually allowed her to get her way but it drove a firm wedge between them. As did the list of additional expenses for this rarefied universe we were entering.

'A hockey stick? Oh, for God's sake!' my mother wailed one night, furtively checking the letter headed 'School Accessories' while my father immersed himself in poetry. She scoured junk shops until she found a battered antiquity from the Fifties, handing me white bandages from Boots to tape over its vintage origins. The expensive ski trip we planned to cry off with fake illnesses, but the brown modesty games knickers, worn to prevent 'unfeminine reveals', were the final straw. 'Shove a white pair in the wash with a dark T-shirt, they're only bloody pants,' she sighed.

The sense of otherness that always lurked within me had been temporarily lifted by the arrival of Jane in our lives and Lynsey next door. I had a novel sense of safety in numbers. But the feeling was about to come rushing back, exploding into something altogether more overwhelming in this rarefied world. We weren't in dog-family country anymore. We were in housekeepers and heated pools country. Our classmates were the children of wealthy captains of industry, some of whom lived behind electric gates. A world that couldn't be exposed to bailiffs and a stripper called Johnny da Silver. Which meant a whole new, epic level of concealment. My occasional trips back to the gentle world of the Simpsons felt like a return to lost innocence compared to this terrifying new terrain.

There was an increasingly fractious atmosphere at home.

'They're rowing,' Rach would say, shutting the door on the raised voices downstairs, turning up Adam Ant on the second-hand custard yellow FisherPrice record player. Rach had opened it with horror on her last birthday, her hopes dashed after months of pestering for a stereo 'like everyone at school!'

She was thirteen now, to my eleven, and drifting into the

arena of floral fragrances, eyeliner and crushes on boys. The whole shared room thing was getting a little old. She often moaned about privacy, locking herself in the bathroom to get away from my childish games and my parents' excess. 'I can't even start my PERIOD in peace,' she said angrily, as my mother and father greeted the news with a celebratory dance and loud chorus of the song 'Congratulations'.

Our regular weekend visits to my grandmother's eccentric lair felt even more surreal alongside our new privileged world. Rach and I began to resent turning down our peers' exciting invitations to burger restaurants and ice-skating trips to honour our 'quality time'. Jane drew a cartoon in a gesture of solidarity, captioned 'Em, Rach and duvets going to Nan's again!' We stuck it on the kitchen pinboard in protest.

Lynsey took Rach and me out to dinner in a local restaurant for 'a girls' chat'. I felt honoured. It was as if we'd become the ladies in *Dynasty*, worthy guests in our own right rather than tolerated children. But then she brought up the subject of my mother's need for 'support' when the pudding arrived, like a private wealth manager delaying the fragile matter of the un-approved loan. And I wondered what was being said in those conversations *à deux* they had in her living room.

Given the constant talk of money problems and the increasingly bad vibes, we weren't prepared for the news my father shared one morning. 'How would you like to go to Germany, girls?' he asked. Noticing our stunned expressions, he swiftly explained that this wasn't an entire life relocation. It was a family holiday. Those things that the organised, forward-thinking dog families had.

'We're going to stay with the Kaiser!' he told us. The Kaiser was a German director friend of my father's, who generously tolerated his offensive nickname. My father had us at the mention of his swimming pool. But lost us with the next revelation. My mother wasn't coming with us.

'Why can't you come, Mum? I don't understand,' I asked, panicking over the prospect of my father's exposure to the complicated details of travel. He struggled to make it back from work without losing his house keys, so the idea of him returning with three intact passports seemed optimistic. But mostly, the whole thing just felt a bit off. Our troupe was a fixed quartet. My mother evened out my father's oddities, smoothed over his interactions with strangers. It was her who talked airport staff into letting us board our flight past the final call. She smelt of amber and warmth and Holly Village. I needed her to come with us.

She mentioned a play she had to finish writing and brightly suggested we buy new outfits for this slightly disquieting trip. 'Just don't tell your father, for Christ's sake!' A week later our new triumvirate headed off to Germany, swiftly rearranging our performance to cover up the absence of our recently departed front woman.

'Why aren't you swimming, Rach?' my father asked, as he and I splashed around in the pool on our first day, with the Kaiser's daughter and glamorous second wife.

Rach was sat in the shade buried in a Jackie Collins novel – which was, I felt sure, the real reason behind his sudden urge to interrupt her.

'I don't want to. I've got a . . . *sore tummy,* Dad,' she said.

Hoping he would understand the twee euphemism our teachers used for periods.

He was having none of it.

'Rachael, you seem to have this curious philosophy that life is designed around what you want. Swimming is good for your general . . . feminine health,' he finished awkwardly. 'I would encourage you to get in the pool.'

The gold swirly font on the jacket of the Jackie Collins novel hit the ground as Rach abandoned her angelic white swan role in a fit of frustration, heading into the house in humiliated fury.

'He doesn't understand about periods and things, Rach,' I consoled, having fled to join her indoors, my damp swimming costume leaving sodden patches on the Kaiser's high-thread-count sheets. I felt smug suddenly in my uncomplicated pre-pubescent body, free from emerging hormones and curious sprouting body hair.

'I miss Mum, you know,' said Rach, sadly. 'I wish she had come with us.'

'Rachael!' I shouted, mimicking my father's formal tones, 'you seem to have this *curious philosophy* that life is designed around what you want!' She smiled at our familiar collusion. But it wasn't enough. Mum just knew how to handle moments like this.

We went for a walk, the next day, in the forest near the Kaiser's house. My father encouraged me to climb on his shoulders. It wasn't something we had ever done before, a confident paternal activity. But I was happy to collude in the performance, as he rose up, crying something about 'standing on the shoulders of giants!' Warming to the audience approval, he began to run while singing 'The Long and Winding Road'.

'Stop it, Dad!' I yelled as he raced through the forest, lost in his reverie.

'Don't worry, darling!' he reassured me before colliding at speed with a fallen branch, sending me flying over his head to land on the muddy ground.

'Dad, you idiot!' yelled Rach, rushing to examine the trickle of blood under my nose and removing the bracken from my hair as I looked up at her in confusion.

My father patted my back guiltily, calling himself 'a twenty-four-carat turd', for once lacking the elegant wit to disguise this moment of drama.

I knew he was embarrassed that his clumsy attempt at normalcy had backfired. He simply didn't have the capacity to park his abstract thinking and pull off a family walk. Without my mother's restraining influence, we were all slightly adrift; just as without his rational analysis, my mother's more emotional nature often sent moments into high drama. It took both of them for our particular family engine to judder along without stalling.

The rest of the holiday passed in better spirits as we made an unspoken decision to seek out things that suited my father's traits better than outdoor pursuits. We bought coloured stationery from a bookshop while he flicked through the Brecht and Kafka, and giggled at German soap operas. Rach and I came home tanned and excited, for once returning holiday-makers rather than bewildered newcomers to a strange country.

'When we get back Mum and I have something to tell you!' my dad said as we made our way down the rain-slicked motorway to north London, the ancient car wipers squeaking like Greek furies.

'What is it? Will we like it?' I asked.

The swell of Stephen Sondheim's dark operetta *Sweeney Todd* thundered out of the car stereo.

My dad glanced over his shoulder at us briefly. 'We'll see!'

Our parents turned off the television for the news my father had trailed in the car. Danny the 'dead pussy' had only warranted a dip in TV volume, but this revelation was getting a total media blackout.

'So, your mother and I . . .' began my father, 'your mother and I . . . we have decided that we are going to separate. For a bit,' he added, the lollipop after the injection.

'What do you mean "separate"?' I cried even though I knew exactly what he meant. I was buying time to absorb the news. In the early Eighties, people's parents separating was a new and scary concept, unusual enough to form the plot of the entire film *Kramer vs Kramer*. It happened to rich people in newspapers, to characters in the American soaps and was addressed in the teen fiction we read. How was it happening to us?

'So that means you've getting divorced,' said Rach bluntly, already making a sophisticated mental leap to a place from which I recoiled. Separation meant maybe, divorce meant definitely.

'We didn't say "divorce", darling, we said . . . separated,'

Mum said. 'Dad needs to be near the BBC so he'll stay with friends. And we thought we could do with . . . a break.'

A break. Breaks were what you had in school. They meant delicious sips of hot chocolate from the vending machine, laughing about boys and singing Madness songs. Breaks were positive, full of possibility. This was ominous and life-altering and shameful. This was no break – it was a hideous rupture.

Rach and I exchanged stunned looks. I decided to hop on board with her teenage cynicism and stop buying what they were selling. I hadn't heard of any other fathers reluctantly abandoning the family home in order to live next door to their work. Especially not work that involved wandering around in socks saying to female colleagues, 'Annabel, you're looking dangerously bewitching today.'

'We asked in the car if it was good news. You said "we'll see!"' challenged Rach, evidently finding it easier to focus on my father's breach of taste rather than the traumatic revelation itself.

'Well,' my dad said, and then paused. 'It could be a preferable outcome.'

There are some phrases you turn around in your head for a long time trying to make sense of the various possible meanings. 'Preferable outcome' would join them.

I began to cry and my mother wrapped me in braceleted hugs. Rach shed angry tears, wiping them away furiously, conned by this news, the lazy plot twist that makes no sense of the preceding action. Except when you replay it, and notice the giant red flags you failed to see all along.

We may have never been a dog family. But now? We weren't even a family anymore.

I had never considered the possibility of our quartet being ripped apart like this by creative difficulties. We laughed off disagreements, we coped and got on with the show like professionals. Our odd tribe of four, with our own language and dynamics, always returned to each other after our adventures into other worlds. How could it all cease to exist?

'Maybe you'll get back together one day?' I offered, with the false hope of the recently dumped, who hasn't grasped that the person delivering the news made their peace with it long ago. There are no deals to be struck, no reprieves. They are just assessing how to get out of this conversation with the least collateral damage.

'Who knows!' my father replied, half-heartedly.

Rach and I went upstairs to put on our pyjamas at the premature hour of 5.00pm. Perhaps we were trying to remind them that we were just kids. We used precocious language, knew never to serve sweet wine and how to talk to the Leader of the Opposition but we were eleven and thirteen. The pyjamas seemed the simplest way to say, 'We're scared.'

Over the next few months Rach and I clung to each other. She reminded me, 'We ALWAYS have each other, Emmy.'

I told her about the girl at our smart school in whom I had stupidly confided. 'That's absolutely GHASTLY!' she had said, before spreading the news everywhere. Our Gaza Strip chats went on all night as we tried to make sense of it, digging into the corpse of the marriage like forensic pathologists.

There was fighting over which parent would move out. My

father described himself as a homeless man trying to con his way into someone else's house. I felt he didn't really want to leave. He moved between friends' spare rooms, spent several months with a TV presenter, had an awkward spell with a male producer who made a pass at him, and a few weeks with a couple who brought him out with the cognac to perform eloquent tricks.

My mother was keen to shield us from some of the more unedifying details of their split and insisted that he visit us every weekend for 'family time'. But in a moment of indiscreet fury, she told us the truth – that he was in love with Anita from the BBC. Anita didn't seem like much of a TV-advert mum anymore. Apparently the affair was over. Anita had an adoring husband who was a rather safer long-term bet than my father.

Mum decided not to name Anita in the divorce papers, saying, 'There's no need for her children to suffer.'

Rach and I imagined their continued blissful ignorance as our lives fell apart.

We never mentioned Anita to my father. And eventually my parents drew a veil of good-natured civility over the whole business. Every weekend my dad dutifully arrived at Holly Village and ate roast lunch as he always had, before returning to his new bachelor life.

My mother, aware that his involvement in our lives required daily stage management, sometimes suggested he took us for a day out. His first attempt saw the three of us drifting around like an aimless teenage gang, until somehow we ended up in a dark alley near Archway tube station. 'There we go, food!' he said, pointing at a strip-lit fast food café.

It was in Burger Delight, over limp chips and warm Fanta, that we learned he 'never really wanted marriage and children.' It was something he had simply fallen into. His eyes filled up as he said that we had nevertheless become 'the only true and good things in this absurd life.' He told us he had no place in the new independent existence my mother craved. And chose not to refer to the extra-marital indiscretion.

A few months later he introduced us to a new girlfriend. The Russian, as we called her, had a townhouse in Chelsea that smelt of incense and was scattered with Tibetan antiques. She made films about human-rights violations, always wore silk underwear to war-torn countries and was friends with both the Dalai Lama and Colonel Gaddafi (whom my mother insisted 'she DEFINITELY went to bed with').

'Do you want frankincense in your slippers tonight, darling?' the Russian asked my father one night as Rach and I sat awkwardly in her kitchen, sipping iced water.

We exchanged wary looks as we witnessed this petite glossy-haired stranger embracing him. I wondered how he could shift his allegiance so openly to someone else. How he could call her 'darling', the word he still used, out of habit, to address my mother. He looked wrong in this exotically glamorous woman's space, with her peaceful Zen garden and pristine white kitchen units. Like a battered typewriter in a new modern office space.

A glossy foreign correspondent should have been the dream companion for someone uncomfortable with commitment – but with two kings sharing a space, the court tends to get a little crowded.

Their relationship foundered after less than a year and descended into a war of hostilities. 'Oh God, the Russian's thrown your father's passport into the Thames,' my mother laughed of the latest drama. She was now just a baffled spectator in his emotional life, much like us.

Some months later, a typed letter found its way onto the Holly Village doormat, addressed to 'Christine, Rachael and Emily'. The words were typed but for a flourish of fountain pen at the bottom that read, 'Anonymous'. It looked like the piece of evidence that would finally nail the sloppy perpetrator in a film noir.

And sure enough, 'Anonymous' had blown their cover with a postmark stamped 'Chelsea'.

'Michael has just become a father for the third time,' Rach read out, sat cross-legged on the sofa. 'The child, Misha, will live with a family retainer in France. THIS child was planned and wanted. Unlike the two YOU blackmailed him with.'

'So Rach and I are the "two YOU blackmailed him with?"' I said.

'Yes.' My mother laughed. 'Charm-ING!'

According to my mother, the Russian had faked a pregnancy, wandering around with a cushion shoved up her dress. 'There is no bloody Misha.'

Misha never materialised but I'll always be grateful to him in spirit. 'The two YOU blackmailed him with' became our sign-off in every card Rach and I ever sent our mother.

The brief domestic constancy in Holly Village (for 'the two SHE blackmailed him with') was about to end. My mother was having strained conversations with 'the bloody Walkers' about rent so we took up a friend's offer to move into their Islington terraced house while they were abroad.

Holly Village had represented a shot at a consistent history. I felt wistful looking at our now empty rooms, stripped of life, as my mother's friends came round with wine and bin bags to transport us to our new temporary home.

Treacle wasn't sold on our new place. He'd traded a magical garden for a tiny patch of urban concrete. He slunk up and down the house's metal spiral staircase, weaving in and out of our three bedrooms, weighing up the safest bet for a long-term bed companion.

One Sunday my father was helping us clear the dishes away after his regular lunch date with us. He began flicking through a catalogue from an art exhibition Rach had saved up to buy.

'Can I borrow this Chagall catalogue, Rach?' he asked suddenly.

'Yeah, sure. Are you all right, Dad?' she asked.

He looked as if he had tears in his eyes. But then my dad often had tears in his eyes when he was immersed in a cultural moment. It wouldn't take much. A TS Eliot poem. A Shakespeare sonnet. An Orson Welles film.

'I'm okay. Love you very much. Both of you. Night, girls.'

And he shut the door behind him.

There were three white envelopes lying on the doormat when I let myself in from school the next day. One said 'Emmy', underlined, in my father's unmistakable handwriting. I began to read it.

Dear Emmy,
By the time you read this I will be on a plane on my way
to start a new life in New Zealand alone. I am sorry not
to have told you in person . . .

It was beautifully written. Of course it was. It was moving. It was almost reasonable. He talked of 'needing to do this for himself', of new job opportunities that would change his fortunes and finally he said, 'I hope you can forgive your old dad one day.'

My mother burst through the door with Rach, juggling bags of steaming fish and chips. 'The queues were round the block! But I couldn't be bothered to cook . . .' She trailed off as she saw my expression.

I handed them the letters. 'Read these. Dad's gone.'

The rest of the night passed in a fog of melancholy punctuated by pockets of hysteria. Aunty Lyn turned up, immaculate and solution-driven, with her chequebook and lawyers' numbers. 'Thank you, Michael,' my mother said at one point. 'I have SEVEN pounds in my FUCKING purse.'

My grandmother arrived in a cab from Brixton, smelling of gin and shouting about her 'connections' at Interpol. 'I don't think that even exists anymore,' Rach whispered to me.

My mother's mature civility towards him, born mainly out of a desire to keep him in our lives, collapsed briefly. She mentioned a 'Maori princess' he was now 'screwing!' (She was in fact a prominent intellectual and activist but it played better to dismiss her as some entitled prima donna.) 'It won't last,' she continued, lighting endless cigarettes. 'They never do.'

Rach and I escaped upstairs to the spare room. It was the place we had begun to retreat to together, a sort of junior common room. We would talk about boys in there, experiment with smoking avocado leaves and listen to Frankie Goes to Hollywood. Rach had recently pulled out my mother's old Beatles albums but I decided we needed the bubble gum comfort of Wham! tonight. We curled up together on the mattress, eating cold chips. Treacle, always dependable in a crisis, nestled between us.

'He took my Chagall catalogue,' Rach said simply.

Apart from the odd postcard and phone call, our father disappeared from our lives for the next five years.

Dog families weren't immune to domestic problems but I felt sure they didn't handle them in this way, like actors slipping out of the stage door while someone else cleared the set. I felt ashamed when my father left. As if somehow Rach and I hadn't been enough to keep him with us. If we had just been smarter, kinder, more loveable, perhaps he would have stayed. People didn't leave you if you were loveable.

'Looks like I backed the wrong horse,' I said to Rach that night. We tended not to voice our respective silent allegiances to each parent, but she laughed grimly in acknowledgement.

I decided not to share the true extent of my pain. Instead I poured out my feelings every night in a diary, scoring my black fury over the pale pink pages. 'Why did you GO? Why did you leave ME?!' I scrawled, retreating into the simple worldview of a toddler. One who didn't know about screwing a Maori princess and divorce and people not wanting children. The sadness and anger eventually settled and began to mutate into something else. A brittleness that attached itself to me, spreading like creeping ivy that cleverly hid my fear and hurt.

But what I hid most of all was how much I missed him.

'Oh bloody GREAT timing!' my mother said.

The owners of our temporary home had announced they were returning. So, we packed up our theatre programmes and moved into a dilapidated two-up two-down in Wood Green. 'But that's an AWFULLY rough area!' one of my friends at our posh school helpfully announced. My mother coped with the 'awfully rough area', known for its high crime rate, by giving Wood Green a camp French moniker, calling it *Forêt Vert*. Treacle attempted to find pals among the world-weary local strays, but the velvet collar gifted to him by James Coburn marked him out like some effete Etonian, unable to blend into his new manor.

The odd loyal *bon viveur* from our old life paid us visits, helping to put up shelves and donating furniture, but the party had come to a screeching halt. We were now just a collection of travelling souls rather than the beating heart of a thriving salon. Jane and her mum Mandy visited, a reassuring reminder of our old lives, bringing laughter and female solidarity. My friendship with Lucy Simpson had tapered off into a family-based connection, but we'd catch up during our mothers' intense chats over wine at their house. Ralph was reliably thrilled to see me, his smell taking me back to a time that I now missed.

The red bills mounted up and we became dependent on loans, Oxfam shops and generous friends. But somehow, through sheer force of will and endless borrowing, my mother managed to keep us at our expensive school. 'I don't want you to end up in my bloody position!' she said.

I began to lie a lot. Mainly to my school friends. I told a girl who lived in a mansion that we had seventeen rooms in our house. I invented a family ski trip we'd once taken. I learned to be vague about where exactly we lived, and forgetful if someone asked where my shoes came from, deciding this was a tough room for 'the Cancer Research charity shop'. I lied about my father, turning him into a doting fantasy figure unavoidably detained on foreign TV shoots. I committed fully to my role as visitor in other people's homes, gracious, courteous and undemanding, hiding the secret of our collapsed family, my absent parent and our empty bank accounts. I felt like north London's answer to the Talented Mr Ripley, waiting to be exposed at every turn. But my new brittle armour came in handy, encasing me in smart-arse cynicism.

I began to imitate Lynsey and those women from *Dynasty*. Formidable, icy, free from messy emotions. Madonna became my new idol. I copied her language, using phrases like 'Don't give me attitude!' and 'Screw you!' My friends daydreamed about romantic weddings with their pop star crushes. My fantasies were revenge dramas involving George Michael cheating on me. 'Congratulations, YOU just lost the best thing you ever had,' was my cool parting shot to him, as he sobbed in his hotel bed, tears dripping from under his aviators.

I envied the way Rach dealt with our new circumstances. She didn't lie about our house having seventeen rooms. She didn't fantasise about George Michael cheating on her. She didn't hide who she was; in fact she was happy to invite over the floppy-haired public schoolboys who were starting to take an interest in her. As if she was miraculously able to separate her worth from parental circumstances. She rejected the affluent world to which I craved membership privileges, going on CND marches, cultivating people outside of our school and dismissing the materialistic scorn of snobbier peers. She blossomed physically into someone the popular girls now viewed as 'actually really pretty!' She was morphing from quiet observer into aesthetically-pleasing Apollonian.

I felt a surge of pride at her newfound acceptance, but Rach seemed uninterested in the people that now held her in high esteem. Unlike me, she had never really deserted our tribe of misfits, holding their maverick code close to her heart.

A year after my dad's departure, when I was fourteen and Rach sixteen, my mother told us that we were all going to be separated for a brief period. She had got a small acting job in Australia, in a touring Samuel Beckett play alongside the actress Billie Whitelaw. She reassured us that it would only be for a few months, which would 'fly by!' Rach and I were going to live with two different families. Rach was to be placed with a director and actor and their two small children; I was to return to dog-family life with the Simpsons.

My mother decided to deal with these circumstances with the optimism of a 1940s musical heroine who adapts to challenges by announcing, 'Let's put the show on in the BARN to raise money for the orphanage!' But whichever way you tried to spin it, our gossamer-thin ties were finally snapping under the weight of our chaos. The dream she had wanted: the kitchen table surrounded by family, the plates of home-cooked lasagne, the sense of belonging, was staying a dream. We were now just four individuals, living in different homes. The show had been cancelled due to ongoing cast absences.

I was finally getting the life I had always wanted – one with a bona fide dog family. But no one had told me the deal meant giving up Rach.

'I don't want us to be split up, Ray,' I cried, as we packed up our clothes.

'It'll be okay, Em. I'll come and see you lots!' she said.

My emotion seemed excessive next to her resigned acceptance. We carried on emptying our things into suitcases, A-ha playing in the background, as I prepared to cloak myself in my gracious, charming guest persona for the next few months, shape-shifting my way into the dog families.

Treacle, the last reminder of our Holly Village stab at domestic consistency, was to be rehomed with my mum's on/off boyfriend. John was an actor who had starred in a 1960s hospital drama. I had seen old publicity shots of him posing with a stethoscope and a lit cigarette. He was a kind but reserved Yorkshireman, someone who popped up when my mother needed him and retreated when she didn't. John was everything my father wasn't, relying on quiet actions over charm, someone who drilled walls and changed tyres. He often retreated into the dialogue of war dramas in which he'd appeared. 'At least all's quiet on the western front!' But I sensed that he was as thrown by my mother's imminent absence as we were.

We waved goodbye to my mother at the departure gate. 'Bye, darlings! I love you so much. It will go so quickly!' she cried, waving frenziedly, before her figure slowly disappeared.

Some nights during those months I spent living in the Simpsons' spare room, with its anglepoise desk lamp and alarm clock courteously provided, I struggled with sleep. The Simpsons were welcoming and supplied a structure I'd never known before. But I missed my mum's theatrical laugh and amber scent. I was nostalgic for my father's amusing insights. Mostly I wanted my sister back by my side, where she belonged.

There were nights when I would creep down the stairs to the Simpsons' pine kitchen, open the freezer and stick a spoon into one of the neatly stacked tubs of ice cream, smoothing the surface afterwards to hide my midnight raid. Then I would quietly head for the utility room and lie down in Ralph's hair-covered bed, stroking his soft fur as he licked my face. He welcomed me each time like an adored long-lost relative. My occasional nocturnal visits were our secret, never to be shared.

Mum called and wrote letters about her adventures in Australia. 'It's NO fun, I can't smile without you – like that Barry Manilow song!' Dad's postcards from the same continent landed on the pristine doormat, saying 'Rotorua is like a tired old drag queen – lots of glitter and paint but faintly suburban underneath.' Rach and I talked every day from our respective temporary homes but kept our chats brief and formal, wary of taking up too much space in the homes of our benefactors.

My mother eventually returned, arriving outside the school gates one day. She wrapped me in hugs, laden down with Koala T-shirts and Australian sweets. 'I have MISSED you like mad!' she said, as we bundled my suitcase into the car to collect our two remaining band members, Treacle and Rach.

Our little house smelt faintly of damp and neglect. The gate had fallen off its hinges, the central heating had broken down and Treacle expressed his joy at being reunited by taking a dump in the living room. But who cared. I was back with Rach.

'Your father's coming back for a visit!' my mother announced two years later. It had been nearly five years since we opened the letters telling us he was leaving the country. I wasn't sure he would recognise the people we had become. Perhaps he'd skipped too many seasons to ever fully catch up.

The concept of parental boundaries had always been sketchy but since my father left, that fragile wall had crashed down entirely. Now that I was nearly seventeen and Rach was nineteen, the three of us had abandoned any pretence at being a family. We were more a bunch of women taking part in a 'Three Girls Go Wild!' reality show. Our relationship with our mother felt volatile, almost adolescent. There were rows about borrowed clothes and stolen cigarettes. Rows with the passionate intensity usually reserved for partners. Nighttime Mum had triumphed over Daytime Mum. Our friendship groups began to blend together: her new collection of gay theatre friends with our teenage pals who came round to smoke dope and drink wine. There was a girls' holiday where Rach and Mum both got off with Spanish waiters. '*Hers* was GROSS, Em,' Rach whispered to me.

So when I heard that my father was returning to London for a brief work trip, I was thrust back into an old world, one that belonged to someone else. I was in a resolutely female gang now and the parts for 'occasional male visitor' had already been allocated.

My mother's on/off boyfriend John was back in our lives and Rach had a new romantic interest, called Zygi. I stuck to the safer, sustained intrigue of 'will they won't they' crushes. I lived through Rach's relationship, attaching myself to the two of them like a pestering sidekick, adopting Zygi's circle of affable teenage friends as my own. I clung to my new identity as 'Rachael's sister', in a reversal of our childhood order. It was a relief to sit back and enjoy the ride on her journey.

The reunion with our father didn't exactly turn out to be the 'lion gets reunited with previous owner' YouTube tearjerker I'd expected.

Publicly I viewed my father with eye-rolling laughter. It worked with my new persona, of junior Madonna in training. But secretly I had written him long letters, looking up words in the dictionary to impress him. 'I brush my hair *laboriously.*' 'The weather is hopelessly *mercurial*!'

When the meeting finally took place, he wasn't begging forgiveness as we magnanimously offered our absolution. It was more like a wary catch-up with an old ex. We talked about jet lag and movies and the cat. The 'Maori Princess' had been swapped for a new girlfriend, a confident flame-haired woman who arrived clutching his hand. Before long she delved into her bag to retrieve a photo album of her two children.

I felt hurt rising up as my dad talked about the hilarious things these mysterious quasi-offspring said, their birthday parties, the trips they'd all taken together.

My mother yelled down the phone at him after the photo

album incident. 'What do you mean MY daughters, they're OUR daughters!' She banged the receiver down and the three of us sat together like flatmates shit-talking a badly behaved boyfriend, slagging off his new world.

A few days later she suggested Rach and I attempt to salvage things without FHW (as we rechristened the flame-haired woman) before he headed back to New Zealand.

I tried to ignore the knot of pain in my stomach when he arrived at the door, one that had stiffened since our reunion. We talked about friends, he complimented us on our clothes and asked Rach about her boyfriend. Was that it? Was he not going to tell us he regretted everything?

He dropped in FHW's children again, telling us something funny the golden son had said.

Rach smirked at me knowingly. I didn't smirk back. Instead I glared at my father and said, 'Nice of you to tell us all about your new kids, Dad.'

Rach looked at me appalled. *Are you out of your actual mind?* My father paused, breathing heavily through his nose like a thoroughbred about to burst into a canter. He started to yell. In a way he never had before. The missiles flew. He was glad he didn't have to live with me. He didn't know how Rach put up with me.

He shouldn't have mentioned Rach. Not unless he wanted me to go nuclear.

'Shall we talk about Anita, Dad? And how Rach "put up with" that? Let's discuss her!'

This was dangerous terrain I had hurtled us into. I smothered my fear with petulance, stormed out of the living room and headed for the bathroom, banging the door shut. But my hands were shaking.

My dad was a benign man who rarely lost it. He snapped at sloppy thinking, got irritated by life admin and sometimes raised his voice when his opinions were challenged. So I wasn't prepared for what happened next.

I heard his footsteps marching across the kitchen towards the bathroom. He thumped on the door. It vibrated with bangs and kicks, and the noise of him throwing his entire bodyweight at it. The tiny lock pinged off as the door cracked off its hinges and crashed into the sink, colliding with bottles and toothbrushes, before hitting the floor with a thud.

I crouched in the bath and stared at him in silence.

His breathing slowed down. He gazed at the shattered door, then at me. He looked horrified at what he'd done.

'What the hell?' Rach shouted, rushing to restore order, clearing up the disaster scene, talking about everyone needing to 'calm the fuck down.'

He seemed almost shell-shocked, mutely seating himself in the living room before finally apologising for his 'unforgivable loss of control.' And by the end of the evening we had gently begun to refer to it with black humour, reframing it as a comic episode. 'The one where Dad kicked the door down.'

Part of me felt guilty that I'd provoked my father into such lawless fury. Another part of me felt relieved, as if this blind rage had somehow proved that he cared.

'Door-gate' became a family joke but the reason behind the incident was never spoken of again. The past, we collectively decided, was a country best avoided.

My dad returned to New Zealand with FHW, but keen for fresh adventure, he came back to live in England on his own a year later.

My mother attempted to reintegrate him into our lives with occasional Sunday lunches and guest appearances at birthday dinners. He began to trouble-shoot documentaries for former BBC colleagues and write TV reviews for *The Times*, which I showed off to friends at my new sixth-form college. It allowed them to think of me as just another person with divorced parents. They didn't need to know about 'the two YOU blackmailed him with' and Colonel Gaddafi. It was probably easier that way.

Our female gang moved into a new house in a quiet suburban street in Muswell Hill. Rach and I finally had our own rooms. 'Great timing, just as we're about to leave for university,' she said, laughing. Treacle dutifully tagged along with our crew, glad to leave the street gangs behind.

I was secretly proud of my defiant moment with my dad. I had confronted him. It was what Lynsey would have done. What my grandmother would have done. Everyone bought my indestructible, fearless warrior schtick – even my mother, who had started to say, 'You remind me of your grandmother!' But even that indestructible warrior couldn't live forever.

It was Nan's neighbour who called to tell us the news. Rach and I entered the scene of our childhood weekends for the last time, followed by Mum. There was the familiar scent of cat food, stale cigarettes and Charlie perfume. Simon and Lucky emerged from the shadows and scuttled away, their glassy-eyed terror even more palpable than usual.

I heard the low murmur of laughter from the TV through the closed sitting room door. It felt grotesque, unseemly. I turned the door handle, with its decades of layered paint. Everything was exactly as it always had been. The brass ashtray on a stand. The African paintings. A copy of the *TV Times* open on the table. A half drunk cup of tea. And lying on the sofa, in her emerald-green nylon nightie, mouth wide open and black with finality, was Nan. Her brow was furrowed, caught forever in the anxiety of sudden pain.

I hugged her voluptuous frame. The grey roots at the temples of her pink hair were coated in hairspray.

We spent the next few days sorting through my grandmother's turbans and cigarette holders, her Weightwatchers booklets, a box of old diet candy called 'Ayds' withdrawn from shops due to the connotations with a deadly new disease, photos documenting her adventures. We deposited the remnants of her extraordinary life into bin liners.

I realised there were probably people we still hadn't told. Her life had spanned so many continents and re-starts, we would never grasp the entirety of it.

'Maybe we should try and track down Grandpa Bayo in Nigeria,' I said.

'In fairness,' said Rach, 'bigamists can't be expected to go to the funeral of every single wife. Have a heart, Em.'

There's an easy way to tell if someone's lying: they repeat your question back to you. It's because they're caught off guard and are trying to buy time. Here's an example.

Rach: Dad, what is going on? Is Treacle still alive?

Dad: What do you mean 'what's going on?' You're asking me if Treacle's still alive?

I didn't know about that tell for lying when my dad said that. Which is a shame as it would have saved us an awful lot of time.

It had been four years since 'the one where Dad kicked down the bathroom door'. He was still in England, renting a bachelor flat in Chiswick from a male colleague who had left its chrome and black interiors for family life.

Rach and I, now twenty-four and twenty-two, were sharing an apartment just up the road from our childhood home, Holly Village. Funny how we'd been drawn back to it. Our ambitious new colleagues at our graduate media jobs had all left behind their history, baffled at the idea of staying tethered to your past. But I knew why we had both gravitated to this place.

My mother was returning to work in Australia for a year but had remembered the small matter of Treacle. Rach and I were told that our landlord wouldn't budge on his 'no pets' rule (a wish we decided to respect given that he was a drugs kingpin doing time for trafficking), so Treacle went to live with my father.

Treacle was fourteen and entering the geriatric phase of life. He dribbled permanently, was doubly incontinent and his once glossy fur had taken on the uneven texture of a velvet sofa subjected to multiple spillages. His breath smelt, his eyes were gunky, his breathing was laboured, but he was still the good-natured reliable guy of old.

A few months after my mother left, Rach suggested we pop over to my father's one afternoon, for a visit. But it seemed to be awfully difficult for Treacle to find an available diary slot. Arrangements were cancelled, messages were swerved, excuses stacked up. We began to feel like pushy journalists hounding a publicist about their client's recent problem with 'exhaustion'.

Treacle was, according to my dad, spending some time at the family vet's, but his mini-break went on for weeks. So we called the vet for a progress report. Mr Hill informed us that he 'hadn't seen Treacle for over a year now.' He sounded a bit like the innkeeper in a horror film who triumphantly reveals that the person you'd just bumped into has been dead 'nigh fifteen summers'.

Armed with this evidence, we decided it was time for some entrapment.

'Dad, is Treacle at Mr Hill's, the vet in Park Road?' Rach asked. We waited for him to plunge into the trap we'd laid.

He fell in headfirst.

'That's odd,' she replied, 'because I called Mr Hill. He hasn't seen Treacle since last year.'

Dad paused. Cleared his throat. Stuttered a bit.

'Did you say Mr HILL? Sorry, I misheard, thought you said Mr MILLS. Another vet, much better this chap Mills.'

Strangely, we could find no record of a vet whose name differed by two consonants in exactly the same road. But the comedy conceit of Mr Mills became our eternal shorthand for my father's tendency to be economical with the *actualité*.

I knew that our indirect attempt to catch him red-handed in

untruths was perhaps not the right way. But after Door-gate I'd decided to revert to colluding in laughter behind his back. By not confronting him over the small things, we were losing any hope of accessing the truth of the big things. Perhaps there were some doors we wanted to keep closed, fearful of the impact when they came crashing down.

We eventually worked out that my father had handed Treacle over to an actress friend straight after my mother left. A fortnight later she'd buried him in the garden with a blanket that 'matched his fur, lovely chestnut brown. I think he'd had enough of all the moving in the end,' she added, keen to rule herself out as a potential murder suspect.

I felt guilty at our collective abandonment of poor old Treac baby, leaving him to end his days with a stranger in an unfamiliar house.

Sometimes Rach and I walked down the hill from our Highgate flat and peered into the gates of our childhood home. I remembered our dusk visits to retrieve Treacle from the cemetery. Looking up at our old bedroom window, I would be plunged into our past – the noisy actors, the smoke, the bubbling casserole dish, the Shakespeare quotes on the walls, Lynsey holding court while Treac baby settled in James' lap. I missed it.

We never had got our dog, that thing which made people stay.

My mother's elderly neighbour had a sign hanging up in her hall written in curly italics on a wooden heart. 'Home is not a place – it's a feeling!' It was the kind of tacky mass-produced high-street sentiment that I enjoyed sneering at. 'Great. Where exactly are you going to sleep?' But secretly, I was drawn to its bland, simplistic folksiness. Whatever we'd had back then, in those Holly Village days, perhaps it did feel like home.

Home for me now was a person rather than a place. The person who had always been at the centre of my world: my lighthouse, enveloping everything in a reassuring glow. As long as Rach was with me, everything would be okay.

Part Two

Giggle

Chapter Seven

It's a bit strange, the day you wake up to find forty has sneakily entered the room without even having the decency to knock. Especially when you have watched your sister's life play out like a romcom directed by Richard Curtis, the kind of movie that makes 250 million at the box office and cloaks people in a warm aura as they emerge into the street, re-living the sunny exchanges and snug closure.

My life felt like Mike Leigh had agreed to direct an episode of *Sex and the City*. (But got fired for being too British and gritty. And depressing.) Mine was the kind of story more suited to midnight viewings on a subscriber-only arts channel with five thousand viewers if the wind was blowing in the right direction. It would have polarised opinion in east London cafés and left people asking, 'What exactly has the central character *learned*, though?'*

---

* Spoiler alert – fuck all.

RACHAEL — THE MOVIE

INT. MOVING TRAIN — MORNING

Autumn 1989. Scenes of picturesque countryside roll past a speeding train window. A passenger, RACHAEL, is wearing a Free Nelson Mandela T-shirt and blue hoodie, lost in the soundtrack of Morrissey's 'EVERY DAY IS LIKE SUNDAY' on a CD Walkman.

The train slows and we see a station sign, 'WINCHESTER'. She struggles to lug her large case off the train. It opens, scattering her possessions everywhere.

> RACHAEL
> (Laughing despite herself)
> Great fucking start, Rach.

INT. ART COLLEGE — DAY

RACHAEL in white jeans and a long-sleeved T-shirt with a kitsch Virgin Mary motif, sketching fashion designs by a sunlit window before a group of students in Nineties-style coloured jeans and Timberlands enter and carry her, giggling, out to the pub.

EXT. LONDON — DAY

THREE YEARS LATER

RACHAEL looking slightly uncomfortable in a peak-Nineties navy trouser suit and Monica-from-*Friends* bob, outside a smart building in London that says FREUD COMMUNICATIONS. She smooths her peplum jacket down, and immediately treads in dog poo.

                    RACHAEL
        Another fucking great start, Rach.

INT. LONDON — NIGHT

RACHAEL and her younger sister EMILY in a loud Soho bar wearing strappy vest tops, combat trousers and hoop earrings. 'CIGARETTES AND ALCOHOL plays in the background. Two men, ADAM and AUSSIE PAL, approach them.

                    ADAM
          What are you drinking?

RACHAEL smiles, sees EMILY chatting animatedly to AUSSIE PAL.

ADAM and RACHAEL exchange grins.

EXT. CHURCH — DAY

FOUR YEARS LATER

RACHAEL, the beaming bride, walks out into the sunshine holding hands with a jubilant ADAM to the soundtrack of Kylie's 'Spinning Around'. EMILY, a bridesmaid in a pale pink dress with a Rachel-from-*Friends* haircut, is chain-smoking and giving AUSSIE PAL, the best man, fierce looks.

INT. HOSPITAL — DAY

RACHAEL is in labour, gripping the bed for support. CHRISTINE and ADAM are close by.

EMILY enters the room in kitten heels and a pink T-shirt with 'I DIDN'T FANCY HIM ANYWAY' on it.

> RACHAEL
> (Reaching for a hospital sick bowl)
> Great shoes, Em.
> (She vomits into the bowl)

INT, NORTH LONDON HOUSE — DAY

RACHAEL, MIMI (AGE 9) and ADAM are in the living room of their home, with its Farrow and Ball colours and mid-century modern furniture. They are opening a crate, and out runs the newest family member, a biscuit-coloured puppy.

> MIMI
> (earnestly)
> I know what I'm calling him — this is Giggle.

INT. HOSPITAL — DAY

RACHAEL in a hospital bed surrounded by ADAM, MIMI, CHRISTINE and EMILY. A baby wrapped in a pink blanket sleeps on her chest.

> MIMI
> (earnestly)
> I know what I'm calling her — this is Beyoncé.

EXT. NORTH LONDON GARDEN — DAY

A sunny June weekend morning. RACHAEL is sat on a garden chair posing with ALBERTA, ADAM,

MIMI and GIGGLE while EMILY takes a picture of the family scene. GIGGLE leaps up suddenly and grabs a dummy out of ALBERTA'S mouth.

> ALL
> (simultaneously)
> GIGGLE!

We freeze-frame on this moment of domestic playfulness that captures the spirit of joyful family life, as we . . .

FADE OUT TO JOURNEY's 'DON'T STOP BELIEVIN'

Meanwhile, playing in screen two . . .

EMILY — THE MOVIE

EXT. BRIGHTON — DAY

Autumn, 1989, Brighton. We hear mournful cellos, over scenes of seaside detritus. A battered yellow Ford Fiesta, its exhaust pipe dangling off, turns into a university campus. A young woman, EMILY, dressed in denim jacket, gets out of the car followed by CHRISTINE and RACHAEL carrying plants, and an anglepoise lamp. EMILY looks up at a banner. 'SUSSEX WELCOMES CLASS OF 1989.' Somebody has crossed out the 'SUS' so it reads, 'SEX'.

> EMILY
> (V/O)
> I couldn't help but wonder . . .
> how long would it take before

> I was wearing tie-dye and saying,
> 'There are three of us in this
> relationship. You, me and your bong.'

EXT. BRIGHTON STREET — NIGHT

> EMILY
> They say that college life is
> hard to leave and impossible to
> forget. What if today's traffic
> offence is tomorrow's beautiful
> moment?

EMILY and her pal POLLY watch appalled as their peers drunkenly use a traffic cone as a megaphone to the sounds of EMF's 'UNBELIEVABLE'.

EXT. EAST LONDON — DAY

EMILY is coming out of a London tube, the sound of cars honking competing with a depressing acoustic violin version of 'I'M EVERY WOMAN' as we take in city landmarks. She is struggling to walk in high heels and a black skirt suit.

INT. SUNDAY TIMES OFFICES — DAY

EMILY is sitting by giant bags of letters on the dirty floor of a mailroom, her heels off, her skirt riding up.

This is not the glossy role she had dressed for. The EDITOR'S ASSISTANT walks in.

> EDITOR'S ASSISTANT
> Are you Emily?

EMILY is relieved, the terrible mistake has
been rectified. She smooths her skirt down.

                    EMILY
          Yes! I'm a graduate, actually,
          so I think there's been some—

                EDITOR'S ASSISTANT
            Yes, you shouldn't be doing
            this at all. The editor needs
        you to wrap his Christmas presents.
        And choose them. And write the cards
                    as well.

INT. LONDON — DAY

A small LONDON apartment. A stripped down,
haunting strings version of 'INDEPENDENT WOMAN'
plays. The empowering lyrics are undermined by
the scene in EMILY'S living room. A discarded
packet of prawn cocktail crisps. An overflowing
ashtray. A stack of unpaid parking tickets.

                    EMILY
                    (V/O)
            You don't choose a city like
        London, it chooses you . . . In this case,
          it chose me a flat containing a family
                of mice and a fridge with two
        bottles of champagne and one eyeliner.
        The first face I saw every morning was
              the old man upstairs, whose kink
          was asking me to tie his shoelaces.

EMILY answers the door to RACHAEL and
CHRISTINE, armed with flowers and gifts for
her new flat. They enter the kitchen together.

CHRISTINE
(conspiratorially to RACHAEL)
The thing is, how will she COPE on
her own? She's always had me to look
after her.

RACHAEL
Remember when Free Willy was
released into the ocean? She'll
cope like he coped, Mum.

INT. TAXI, OUTSIDE EMILY'S FLAT — NIGHT

EMILY
(to the DRIVER)
I've lost my purse. And . . .
shit. My keys.
(She glances across the road)
Fuck, my CAR'S been clamped?
(Slurred)
Listen, have you got a phone
I can borrow?

INT. EMILY'S FLAT, CHRISTMAS EVE — DAY
EMILY is opening a present from THE COMIC, her
boyfriend. It's a pink toy mechanical poodle.

EMILY
I love it!

THE COMIC
Until we get a real one.
I think they come in pink.

INT. EMILY'S FLAT, THREE MONTHS LATER — NIGHT

EMILY is throwing the pink poodle in the bin

and necking wine, watched by RACHAEL. There's
a knock at the door. EMILY sighs with relief.
He can't live without her. He's back.

> OLD GUY UPSTAIRS
> (pointing to his shoes)
> Would you mind, love?

EMILY taking boxes into her new garden flat
helped by ADAM, RACHAEL and CHRISTINE.

> EMILY
> (V/O)
> Maybe some of us just aren't
> cut out for life with a Labrador
> and a people carrier. And maybe that's okay.
> Just as long as you find a place to live
> where old men don't regularly
> ask you to tie their shoelaces.

> RACHAEL
> You've got a little garden!

> EMILY
> I can get a dog!

> MIMI
> You always say you'll get a dog.
> But you never do.

MELANCHOLY CELLO MUSIC AS WE

> FADE TO BLACK

2010

I looked at the picture Rach had texted me: 'Meet Mr Giggle. He has a diamanté collar and a satin cushion. Campest dog you'll ever meet. xx'. This puppy wasn't just cute, he was all set to one day break Instagram. He had giant Disney eyes, a tilting head and soft butterscotch coat. Another text arrived, of nine-year-old Mimi holding up her prize. She had a hint of triumphant glee in her eyes, that said, 'Persistence is the difference between no and yes. Have you not read *The Art of the Deal*?'

The arrival of Giggle, this tiny half-pug half-chihuahua, was weighted with significance. Rach had finally joined the dog families, with their gentle order, bulging fridges and puppy treats in kitchen cupboards. The home she'd created was a thoughtfully decorated haven, frequented by friends popping in for rosé as their children shrieked happily with Mimi in the garden.

But there were bursts of our old life to remind her of how far she'd travelled. My father popped up occasionally as an amiable uncle figure, and brought his customary eccentricity.

'I'll cut Mimi's birthday cake!' he once offered, but halfway through the task got distracted by a Martin Amis book. 'Dad,' Rach said gently, 'you left the carving knife on Mimi's trampoline. Also you're leaning against the hob. Your jumper's now on fire.'

Mr Giggle the chug somehow helped diffuse moments like this – he managed to lend chaos a benign charm. He benefited from the good-natured stoicism of the pug as well as the sociable playfulness of the chihuahua. He reminded me of my sister, in the way his orthodox prettiness disguised a maverick spirit.

'Giggle! You're not meant to be up here!' Rach would say half-heartedly as he jumped up to what was known as 'Rach's corner' on the couch. He covered her in puppy bites, staring at her in awe like the boyfriend who knows he's punching above his weight.

I would watch Rach putting on his harness and lead, bending down to give his tummy a rub as his bubblegum-pink tongue panted dementedly. I felt a pang of envy as she grabbed poo bags and wrapped up in a scarf to honour his nightly bathroom break. She spoke the language of the other dog owners now, one rooted in dutiful routine.

Giggle was far more than a dog. He was the embodiment of the path in the woods Rach had chosen, the one signposted 'National Trust Picnic Area'. In contrast to the one I had taken, marked 'Danger! You are in Bear Country.'

Rach had flirted with instability in her early twenties, but it was the harmless sort tied to youthful exuberance, not the lingering kind that keeps you on the party train beyond your stop. She had a few dalliances with mercurial artists but chose a future with Adam, a Mancunian advertising creative who made her laugh and wasn't afraid of commitment. She found herself working in PR, which allowed her to draw on the skills we'd learned as childhood apprentices – racking up our ten thousand hours at my parents' academy dedicated to the study of charm.

'Rach is such a talented artist, I do wish she was still painting,' my mother sometimes lamented. But if you wanted estate cars, puppy bowls and roaring fires, you weren't likely to find them in the Van Gogh household.

I was heady with joy on her wedding day. As we sat in the living room of Mum's house, sipping champagne and immersing ourselves in pre-bridal hysteria, it felt as if she were crossing the Rubicon into a new world. It was only subsequently that a sense of deep loss crept up on me. It was as if a limb had been disconnected, and it was difficult to adjust to life without it. I concealed this in case people thought I was just jealous. It felt to me more like the panic of a child losing a parent in a department store, when the world suddenly seems vast and frightening.

I used to compare our intense bond to some of the dog-family brothers and sisters we knew. They seemed to enjoy a slightly more relaxed relationship. The 'how's it going, mate?' siblings, we called them, who enjoyed affable catch-ups at birthdays and Christmas. Perhaps it made life simpler not to speak twice a day and have giggling fits as profound as your passionate rows. Even as adults we were capable of savage brawls. They were documented in our back catalogue like episodes of *Friends*. 'The one where I stole her lilac jumper.' 'The one where I didn't make her a cup of tea and she called me "a selfish bitch", and I called her "fucking unhinged".' 'The one where I bought her tickets to see Boy George and she was too drunk to sound sufficiently grateful, so I dropped her calls for days.'

Our relationship hadn't changed since childhood – she

remained the voice of adult reason in the face of my impulsive unpredictability. 'What's happened, Em?' she would ask calmly when I called her in tears over a bust-up with a boyfriend or a work drama. She was the only person who really knew just how fragile I was underneath my sunny exterior. In a louder way, I fulfilled the same role for her, rushing passionately to her defence, trying to fix things that went wrong in her life, the gatekeeper of her childhood vulnerabilities.

Mimi arrived a year after she got married, a physical mini-me of Rach, with a similar maverick streak. She christened her dolls 'Scrubber' 'and 'Dolly Stump' and occasionally lapsed into a theatrical vernacular picked up from my mother. 'You have made this room look JUST wonderful!' she would say of Christmas decorations. 'Your perfume is absolutely OUT OF MY world!'

When some people reach their desired destination, having chosen a life that hits all the traditional beats, they view those that haven't as exotic curiosities. When people said to me, 'So do you not WANT children then?' or 'Any MAN news?' they were simply addressing the confident, independent person I pretended to be. They didn't know I would store these questions away as judgments.

Rach urged me to dismiss what she called 'the Aga interrogations.' 'I hate it when people say, "I'm SO glad I'm not out there!"' she sighed. 'Everyone is always "out there" – none of us know what's round the corner.'

But I thought that kind of comeback would make me sound brittle and unlikeable. So I laughed at the Aga interrogations and swerved the subject back to the other person, where it was safe. The sense of being 'other' was just part of me, a quirky characteristic like my twisted little toe or inability to be on time. An unfortunate truth that I preferred not to discuss. I saw my life entirely through other people's aspirations and punctuation marks. And in their eyes I was hopelessly off course, doomed to end up wearing moon pendants, clutching a mug that said, 'I'm the crazy aunty everyone warned you about!'

I became so good at concealing my real feelings with perfect make-up and smart remarks that the Aga people thought I was tough and acerbic and happy. They didn't know that I felt scared of the exposure that came with a true union of lives. They didn't know that I saw parenthood and settling down as something I could only consider when I had sorted out my own damage. And in truth, I just never had.

My relationships lurched from one unsuitable match to another. I sought out quick-witted, high-status partners who were always tantalisingly unable to commit to me. (Hi there, Dad.) But the ostensible reasons for the endings – not over their ex, not ready to settle down and several remixes of 'it's not you it's me' – allowed me to avoid the one common factor. Me. When you are simply a collection of the qualities you think people want you to be, when you can't show someone what really frightens you or what pain you have inside your heart, then you are unable to form a true connection with anyone.

My first flat was not a home, more, as one boyfriend, Joel, observed, 'Just a place to rest your head.' So I installed myself as a permanent guest at my best friend's house.

I fell happily into the cocoon of warmth and laughter Jane had created in her own life. She told me she had known she was going to marry her husband, Jonathan Ross, the moment she met him. The things that made her different, seemed to be qualities he celebrated. I became godparent to their children Betty, Harvey and Honey and buried myself in their lively home, becoming an honorary family member. Their household had all the charm of the world I'd grown up in, but was founded on permanence.

And dogs. I didn't know you could make a dog family like this, one with quirks as well as roots. I felt a rush of belonging when the barks subsided as the Ross family dogs recognised their fellow pack member and rushed to greet me. Harvey's expressive-eyed Boston Terrier, Yoda, who lifted his paw on to your hand every ten seconds to indicate, respectfully, that he really needed your full attention. Honey's alpha-female chihuahua, Princess, who attached herself to you possessively, snuffling with smug triumph when she saw off the others for full lap rights. Betty's fluffy, sweet-natured Shih Tzu, Captain Jack, with his curious centre parting. Jane's gremlin-like Brussels Griffon, Sweeney, who followed her around like a devoted but suspicious lover, and Mr Pickle, Jonathan's fabulously eccentric and slightly pot-bellied black pug.

I threw myself into the dazzling whirl of the Rosses' social life, enjoying my role as charming co-host. I was finally a fellow, loved gang member rather than the noisy freak always taking up too much room.

Some people who viewed them solely through the prism of their fame found it difficult to make sense of the space I occupied in the Rosses' lives. 'You've got your feet under the table there,' one woman said archly, when they gave me a generous birthday gift. But Jane was simply my history, a person who had seen me before I strapped on all my false armour. I had a tendency to run away from friendships when minor conflicts arose, but Jane and I were in it for the long haul.

Rach, immersed in her own family life with Adam and Mimi, enjoyed vicarious updates on my adventures: the impromptu weekend hanging out with Russell Crowe where a writer whispered at dinner, 'Sorry, but Nicole Kidman is on my left – hope you understand if I don't talk to you much!' The unexpected evening with Morrissey where I panicked about how to address him. 'Moz, please,' his publicist advised. The time I let myself into Jonathan's dressing room and answered the door to Jim Carrey, offering him champagne and stuffing myself with chocolates before he gently pointed out that I was actually in *his* dressing room.

I was once described as a 'girl about town' in *Heat* magazine, as if I were an It girl rather than someone who often resorted to prayer at cashpoints. I felt sure that 'girls about town' didn't change into red carpet outfits in a Starbucks disabled toilet, using a Sharpie pen to colour in scuff marks on their heels.

I had chosen a salaried career doing jobs in newspapers and magazines because it provided the buzz of the creative world I had grown up in without any of the performer's unpredictability. And because that was just what someone from a middle-class north London family did. It would sound right at dinner parties. I wanted to be around excitement but not the risky focus of it; the sage judge of things, not the curio being judged. 'Em's a trainee at the *Sunday Times*!' my mother would proudly update her friends. 'Em's now Editor-at- Large at the *Evening Standard Magazine*!' 'She's going to be Deputy Editor of a fashion magazine!'

In truth, I was too easily distracted and anarchic for the level-headed routine of an office dedicated to delivering information on a regular schedule. I struggled to concentrate, tried to use humour and presence of mind to get by, and threw myself into my work's exciting social perks instead.

With some jobs, you get to pretend you have a champagne lifestyle on a discounted Prosecco salary. Like my parents, I was a bit chaotic with money in my younger days. There were unpaid parking tickets scattered around my car and I viewed brown envelopes as too much information. But when you work for magazines you get to immerse yourself in a pretend world for brief periods, which is fabulous – as long as you don't forget that it's not actually yours.

Advertisers and fashion brands want you to say nice things about their product, so they spoil you. They fly you First Class to attend fragrance launches, and install you at the Beverly Hills Hotel, with a driver at your disposal, and leave gift bags containing £300-moisturisers in your room.

In return for all this you agree to play the role of an immaculate fantasy guest. A *Devil Wears Prada* character. You wear borrowed Chanel, which means you learn to dodge waiters carrying trays of red wine. You accept compliments on your Louis Vuitton bag, which you were loaned because the label want you to look the part on their front row. And when the bill for dinner arrives you half-heartedly reach for your card, knowing they'll protest. Which is handy, because you need to pay the London Borough of Haringey roughly that amount for council tax.

Sometimes you get taken to Montenegro on a private jet with the world's highest-paid male model, David Gandy. You appreciate him not flinching when your Oyster card falls out on to the carpeted aisle. And you are grateful that the immaculate hotel staff didn't remove you when they discovered Superdrug hairspray in your ensuite.

The job involves regular bursts of essentially harmless 'dress up and pretend' moments. Which have nothing to do with your real life. But to appreciate this, you need something solid to return to, an anchored life waiting for you at home. My colleagues mostly seemed to be able to file these extraordinary moments away in a box marked 'Crazy experiences!' But I often crashed down from them. The life I came back to felt empty. I didn't know where that fashion person ended and I began. I felt jealous of pretend fashion me, who always said the right thing and wore the right clothes. I knew I wasn't especially fulfilled but I didn't have the courage to think about the life I really wanted.

Then I got to know the comic, Frank Skinner.

Frank had been a regular member of our gang at the Rosses'. I had always liked him – when Frank arrived it felt like someone had thrown a handful of glitter into the room. He had settled down recently with his girlfriend, Cathy, and the three of us had become close pals. I would pop over to Frank's flat and we'd eat takeout sushi and drink tea, talking long into the night. We would also watch a lot of trashy TV. 'CATH!' he'd shout, 'get off the toilet. You're missing *Dog The Bounty Hunter*!'

Frank gave tough but useful romantic advice. 'You can never be friends with someone once you've seen their genitals.' And life advice. I sometimes felt he was hinting at a potential I should have the courage to explore. 'You wonder how many beautiful experiences dwell outside our comfort zones,' he once told me, mysteriously.

I didn't expect to get the email that arrived from him one morning. He wanted me to co-host a radio show with him. The heady ego boost was swiftly followed by total panic. He'd got me all wrong. I sneakily stole focus – I didn't nakedly demand it. I was the travelling player who weaved in and out of others' narratives, being charming.

I feared becoming the person my mum had once called a 'dreadful show-off'. I'd discovered that phrase in a letter she sent to my grandmother. (It was the 'dreadful' that stung – look, at least call me an *accomplished* show-off.)

But Frank carried me along on the tidal wave of his enthusiasm.

I was a bit shit at first, settling on a sidekick character for myself, a sort of high-maintenance London snob. But he encouraged me to slowly shed the act and be more authentic. 'Don't feel you have to hide your intelligence,' he'd say. 'Don't tell me stories beforehand, or I won't react genuinely.' It was a crash course in the right way to approach performing. But it was also a bit of a crash course in life.

Frank's fearless honesty as a comic extended with wild abandon into his everyday life. There was no Photoshopping of sometimes harsh truths, no attempt to hide the messier aspects of humanity. 'You can spend your whole life trying to be popular,' he often said. 'But at the end of day the size of the crowd at your funeral will largely be dictated by the weather.' Frank was in many ways my opposite. He served up his beliefs raw without pausing to wonder what people might think or feel. And he talked of 'doing to the world rather than letting the world do to you.'

The Saturday breakfast show on Absolute Radio became a symbol of something important in my life. A place where I could unleash the dreadful show-off for a bit. I formed a bond with our other player – a brilliantly talented stand-up called Gareth Richards – and enjoyed my rapport with the fabulously dry comic who followed him, Alun Cochrane. Our producer, Daisy, became a close pal, our post-show chats evolving into exciting nights out as we threw ourselves into the adventures provided by this new world. It was a place where an inability to blend in was seen as an asset. Even my mum defied the habit of a lifetime by setting a curious contraption called 'an alarm' every Saturday for 8.00am, to listen.

Rising before midday wasn't the only way in which my mum had changed. The credit cards had been cancelled, Harrods food hall had been swapped for Sainsbury's own brand and the bills had shifted from the hostile 'DO NOT IGNORE!' to the respectful, 'Thank You For Early Payment.' She threw herself into the role of grandparent, curating a book called 'MIMI'S SAYINGS' and making her dog family boiled eggs for tea. The turbulent wandering, the mountain of unpaid bills, the rootless existence – none of that, I could see now, had ever been her choice. She had simply jumped aboard a ship with someone who hadn't anticipated passengers.

But in a curious way she'd come to depend on that role of fixer she fulfilled for my father. She still wrote letters to the Inland Revenue on his behalf and helped him sweet-talk angry creditors. Despite her boyfriend John coming over for weekly visits.

'Do you think that being the child of an alcoholic has made you a bit co-dependent with Dad, Mum?' I once asked her, perhaps unwisely.

'Well, that's one way of describing kindness, I suppose!' she said, slightly hurt.

I sensed that she struggled to let go as Rach and I pursued our own lives. One year, when Rach decided to celebrate her birthday with friends in a bar instead of with the usual maternal dinner, my mother phoned in tears, telling us she'd driven to the bar and sat in the car outside. 'I had to know where my daughter spent her birthday.' She seemed sad if we did things without her.

She made great efforts to wheel my father out for occasional lunches, talking about 'family' with a slightly heartbreaking defiance. We collectively indulged in performances for his visiting relatives, and friends. He would tell his engaging stories and chuckle at Mimi's malapropisms. He was never going to be one of those fathers you called about a motorway route, or for mortgage advice. He was still prone to absenting himself for long periods when a new woman entered his life, and always struggled with the whole truth. But he could offer profound insight into the psychology of a misbehaving boyfriend. And tell you, perhaps less usefully, which sanatorium Kafka spent his last days in.

He kept up the revolving door of educated, smartly-dressed brunette girlfriends, to whom we were sometimes introduced. There was the slightly imperious French one, then the actress who seemed way too ballsy to hang around for long, and Richard Burton's widow, Sally, who swept him up into her rarefied world where ladies were shown menus without prices. 'He's trying to keep up with her,' my mum sighed, when he turned up one day with a new car, a gold credit card and an Italian silk tie.

Then finally he got together with a widow whom he'd met via a dating agency. 'He's insisted she call her dog Plato,' said Rach. 'Of course he has.' I laughed.

It was odd to think that even my domesticity avoidant dad had ended up with something resembling the dog-family experience.

I took my desperate longing for a dog into adulthood, boring friends incessantly with my 'plans', which we all knew were the chocolate-fireplace kind. People gave me glossy coffee-table books called *The World of Dogs* – my very own canine porn. I would stop to pet people's terriers in the street with a needy intensity. 'Well, we'd better be getting on then,' they would eventually say, as if they were trying to round off that dutiful coffee with an exhausting friend.

Every time I got close to dog ownership, I bailed. There were too many reasons for it not to work. Who would look after the dog when I was at the office? What if I picked one with a horrible personality? What would the neighbours say if it barked? What if it died?

Of course, I never told anyone the real reason I didn't get a dog – which was simply that I didn't think I was good enough to look after anything.

Sometimes I went with Mum and Rach on a walk to the woods with Giggle, enjoying the pit stops to chat to other dog owners, the joy on children's faces when they patted his head and Giggle's delight as he bounded around, investigating the world.

Twelve months later, Rach's second daughter, Bertie, was born. The Richard Curtis movie had finally come to its jubilant, heartwarming conclusion.

And then, something terrible happened.

Chapter Eight

5 December 2011

'I can't shift this baby weight, Em. It's all just here.'

Rach grabbed her stomach and frowned in the Top Shop changing-room mirror. The teenagers talking about boys in the booth next door were competing with the thumping bass overhead.

My sister had always been a great clothes-shopping companion. It takes someone who loves you unconditionally to deliver those necessary slams of sartorial tough love. We enjoyed our outfit rap battles. 'That top's a bit "Ibiza raver who now has a stall in Camden Market," Em,' she would say. Or, 'Don't like the belt on that coat. Bit "Seventies French Resistance film."' It was all hugely specific. But on this occasion I thought she was being hard on herself. I reminded her that she was forty-three, had a ten-month-old, and we were trying on clothes targeted at people who viewed the Spice Girls like the Golden Girls.

We had our annual conversation about Mum's birthday. My

mother took birthdays very seriously. For her they were ceremonial events invested with huge significance. Often Rach and I ended up having tense disputes about the plans. I usually selected somewhere ritzy and fashionable in central London. Then Rach counter-offered with a rustic, unassuming local restaurant. It was a battle of lifestyles that came to the surface every December. But Rach abandoned the battlefield this time. She was exhausted from juggling work and two kids, I could tell. She said anywhere would do.

Three days later, the three of us met at Bob Bob Ricard, next to the headquarters of my radio show. It was an Art Deco den of opulence, all brass rails, navy leather banquettes and vigilant waiters. There was a little bell in each booth that said 'Press for Champagne.' I thought the camp, Gatsby-esque decadence would appeal to Mum. She made full use of the champagne button and called the fish pie 'absolute paradise!' But Rach pushed her chicken around with a fork, explaining that she was off her food.

'You still can't shift that flu bug, darling, can you?' Mum sympathised, stroking her arm and suggesting we call it a night. 'Well, what a wonderful treat it has been,' she said, 'to be taken to a beautiful restaurant by my two beautiful daughters.'

Suddenly, Rach started to cry. 'I'm so sorry, guys,' she said. 'I don't know what's wrong with me. I feel like shit with this virus. I'm sick of it.'

It was out of character for her to collapse publicly like this.

'Darling, you have two children, a house to run and a job.

You're overwhelmed. Your body can't take it. Let's get you to the doctor tomorrow,' Mum insisted.

We abandoned our search for cabs and got on the tube at Piccadilly. It was heaving with office partygoers and smelt of tobacco, white wine and liberally applied sweet fragrance.

'Can my sister sit down? She's not well,' I asked a middle-aged man.

He nodded politely, offering his seat.

My mother smiled at me approvingly. I caught Rach trying to conceal a grin, amused by my impromptu moment of deference for her. It was kind of not what we did. A polite gesture that belonged to the 'How's it going, mate?' siblings.

17 December

I was on my way to Jane and Jonathan's house for the Comedy Awards, juggling deodorant and false-eyelash glue in a cab, when Mum called. She told me in a surprisingly calm tone that Rach had gone to hospital.

'Hospital?' I repeated. 'What's happened?'

My mum only indulged in drama outside of a genuinely dramatic situation. In a true moment of unexpected upheaval, she was full of firm resolve and optimism. She said it was just a nasty infection: the doctor had diagnosed hepatitis but it was worth exploring further. Rach probably just needed rest and antibiotics.

I was preparing to make phone calls to Jane cancelling tonight when Rach texted me.

In hospital but just infection. GO TO THE COMEDY
AWARDS! No drama. Come tomorrow. And bring me
pants! And charger. Love you xx

My unease was down to the entirely foreign nature of this experience. Rach had always been the safe fortress from the frequent drama of our family life. Not the instigator. But her characteristically light-hearted updates throughout the night put my fears to rest.

A very camp male nurse, a bit like Gok Wan, has been
pushing me in wheelchair xx

Old lady in bed opposite ranting about seeing pieces of
cheese fighting. It's gonna be a long night xx

I arrived the next day with magazines and pants and a stack of Percy Pig sweets. She wanted to hear all the gossip from the night before. Adam was away in New York on a work trip and had decided to fly back. 'I'm sure it'll all be fine,' she said. 'I just hate not knowing what it is.'

The doctors suggested it was best to keep her in over Christmas, to monitor the infection. She had constant fevers and was feeling weak. They thought it might be something to do with her liver.

'Liver? But you don't drink or take drugs,' I said, slightly outraged.

'Exactly, a bit George Best, isn't it,' she said, and smiled, closing her eyes to absorb the cool breeze of the fan.

Adam arrived, full of positivity and reassurance. Rach reached her hand out for him often, and I was relieved that she had a co-pilot to navigate her through this mystery ailment. He used the pronoun 'we' rather than 'you' when discussing her virus. As in, 'We'll feel better when we know what it is.' These were the times when dog families came into their own.

25 December

We had decided to transfer Christmas to the hospital ward. 'Rach is hosting Christmas for us!' my mother declared brightly, her Blitz spirit kicking in.

Rach assessed the lacklustre hospital Christmas decorations. 'Where is tinsel more depressing, do you think, in a hospital or an insurance office?'

My father decided to join us. Adam brought Mimi and Bertie to complete the family visit.

I was aware that Rach had conflicted feelings about whether or not to expose the girls to the potential confusion of seeing her in hospital. And I thought I knew why. When your own childhood had seen you propelled into puzzling adult conversations, when you could recall how you craved routine and certainty, perhaps it was an instinctive urge to want to shield your own children from drips and hospital wards.

We gathered round Rach's bed, my mum wielding carrier bags bursting with curly magenta ribbons and metallic bows. She enveloped Rach in hugs, and arranged flowers. Adam carried a smiling Bertie, and Mimi followed behind him clutching bags of presents. She took in her mother's scrubs and drip.

My father stood by the bed, not really sure how to be. His

coat stayed buttoned up, messenger bag worn across his torso like mittens tied through a toddler's anorak. It was a strategy to combat an absent-mindedness that had recently evolved into early-onset Alzheimer's.

Rach and I had been to the doctor's the previous month, to discuss his diagnosis. As we chatted over scrambled eggs in the café where we discussed the next steps I felt the relief of shared sibling responsibility.

He mumbled to himself by Rach's bedside, rehearsing his words before committing them to public scrutiny, something he had always done, even before the diagnosis. Determined to nail the performance.

Rach was too tired to open the presents. She drank some juice and I peeled a satsuma for her, a little ritual we had developed, which made me feel useful. Adam handed Bertie over to Rach and she bounced her up and down, making silly faces and kissing her.

I suggested doing a video on my phone, so we would be able to look back on that weird December we all spent in hospital. I wanted Rach to have a record of Bertie's first Christmas. We all delivered Happy Christmas messages. Dad woofed at Bertie, and Rach caught my eye. 'Our father has just woofed at my baby,' she whispered, 'and I'M the one on heavy medication?'

'I've got a hair appointment a couple of days after Boxing Day,' I told her. 'Do you mind if I get here a bit later in the afternoon?'

'Of course not. I'm jealous, look at my Courtney Love roots!'

I smiled. I had bought her a voucher from my hairdressers for Christmas, for when she was up and about again. And I would look back and torture her over this particular episode. 'The one where Rach made us eat canteen turkey rolls for Christmas.'

28 December

I was in the hairdressers when Adam called me.

'Em?'

His voice sounded fractured, like cracked paint on a derelict building.

'How's Rach?'

His composure broke.

I rushed through the salon doors out into the chilly Soho street. Rain spat down on me, blending with thick molasses hair dye, which started to trail down my temples.

'What's happened, Ads?'

'She's got cancer, Em. They've found cancer in her liver.'

His voice softened the second time he said the C-word. As if it were too toxic to pronounce.

Something shot into my stomach, a wrecking ball of pain. Not the usual jolt of hurt dismay that crashes in when you hear unpleasant news: a boyfriend telling you 'it's just not working', or a boss saying, 'we've come to the end of the road.' This intrusion felt entirely foreign. The wrecking ball had lodged itself there. It was not a temporary visitor. It was part of me now. It was simply going to have to develop a decent working relationship with the other organs.

We were in that featureless haze between Christmas and New

Year. Tense commuters had been replaced with carefree shoppers and lunch parties. I watched families coming out of Japanese restaurants, high on sugary puddings and the heady seasonal freedom from responsibility. The fairy lights in the window opposite glittered menacingly.

Rach had cancer.

I focused on trying to breathe. I had heard people use the phrase 'I couldn't breathe!' to describe receiving bad news. I'd always assumed it was a slightly overblown statement designed to emphasise shock. Like, 'My world turned on its axis,' or 'I practically died.' But then, I had never imagined receiving news this frightening.

'How bad is it?'

'They're going to tell us more tomorrow. She's taking some diazepam to calm her down. She wants to see you.' His voice broke. 'Come to the hospital, Em.'

This didn't sound like one of the cancers with inspirational survivors' stories and ribbons and midnight walks and high-profile ambassadors. It sounded unalterable.

I walked slowly back into the hairdressers, trying to recall what it felt like to be the person who walked out a few minutes ago. My pre-wrecking-ball self.

Rom, the sweet young colourist, put his arms around me when he saw my face.

'It's my sister, she's got cancer, Rom,' I said, watching tears blend into stray globules of hair dye on the black nylon cape. 'I have to go.' I ripped off the robe.

'It's okay,' he soothed me. 'We're all here for you. Maybe I should just wash the colour out quickly, before you go?' he added, not unreasonably, negotiating with someone temporarily not of sound mind.

I followed him to the basin, focusing on the glossy shots on the wall while the water ran over my head. A heavily lipsticked woman with a geometric chromium yellow bob. A mixed-race model with a deep burgundy crop. I felt a wave of shame that I was in the hairdressers when I found out. 'What did you do today, Em?' 'Got my roots done. How about you, Rach?' 'Got diagnosed with cancer.'

I jumped in a black cab. One of my closest friends, Polly Vernon, who had been a loyal pal since we met at university, had texted me to ask how Rach was doing. She had been offering me daily support through this unsettling hospital stay of Rach's, dropping everything to meet for drinks, providing the distraction of laughter. Just as my lifelong friendship with Jane now wrapped me in a comforting blanket of love, my twenty-year friendship with Polly made me feel rooted and safe. I had told Polly all sorts of extraordinary things in texts. Describing the strange bedrooms I'd woken up in. And the appalling things I'd done.

But I couldn't tell her this in a text reply.

Polly picked up instantly.

'Rach has cancer,' I told her.

The elderly cab driver looked up in his mirror and then averted his glance respectfully.

Polly said, 'Rach will beat this. It's going to be okay.'

I decided to believe her.

When I got to the hospital, Adam and Mum were sitting by Rach's bedside. She was in pink scrubs, blonde hair messily

contained in a ponytail, her eyes slightly glassy from diazepam.

I ran to hug her. I had been determined not to cry but it was
hopeless. I couldn't hide anything from Rach.

'It's really bad, Em, isn't it? Cancer,' she said with a composure
that floored me, staring at me with those familiar cornflower-
blue eyes framed by infuriatingly perfect eyebrows. 'Great brows,
Ma'am,' a scent-sprayer once whispered to her at a New York
department store before he spritzed her with perfume. We said
it to each other all the time now.

We also called each other 'C'. *Catch you later, C.* *Love you,
C.* I'm afraid it stood for the other offensive C-word, the one
that threatens sensibilities rather than lives. It was something
we'd picked up from a book written by my friend David Baddiel:
'C' was the ironically affectionate way the central character
greeted his brother.

I wanted to put my arm around Rach and say, 'Come on,
C! We'll be okay.' But that sardonic, Gen X language felt
redundant. I didn't know how to speak to my sister when she
had just been told she had cancer. I couldn't call her 'C'. It felt
wrong.

The hospital staff had treated us with head-bowed reverence
since the cancer diagnosis. They cordoned off a two-bed area
in the ward so that Rach could have privacy and Adam could
stay over. Rach's phone pinged with messages from friends
who were finding out that she was in hospital but were
unaware that it was anything serious. 'How you are doing?'
'Hoping all ok!' There were abundant XXXXXs on each text.
I tried to imagine what it must be like to be in their place of

sunny ignorance. A nasty virus. A horrid infection that laid her low.

Rach asked me to call some of them. I seized the task. I needed to be useful, to wipe out all the times I had shouted at her. To erase the memory of stealing her Sony Walkman and not telling her for three months. To purge my guilt at once refusing to drive her into the courtyard of her flats and leaving her at the roadside entrance 'because it was too hard to reverse.' Even though she was carrying heavy shopping. And had Mimi with her. What a shitty thing to do.

My mum talked brightly about family members who had overcome cancer, on my dad's side. We didn't mention Aunty Julie, who died of it when she was around Rach's age. My mum was almost manic. She evidently couldn't allow herself to go to a place where this might not work out.

I rang the friends one by one, as Rach looked on. They were shocked. Some offered hopeful spins, survival tales. It's something we all do when someone is faced with bad news; we pull out a comparable experience to express empathy. Not realising that the other person's new world can't yet accommodate anyone else's story. One friend rallied, 'Cancer has so many positive outcomes now! She can have chemo?'

Over the previous hour I had discreetly Googled every variation of the words 'liver' and 'cancer'. I had found articles that began, 'Cancer that has spread to the liver has an extremely poor prognosis.' The words 'five-year survival rate'. I put the websites out of my mind. Frank had always advised against reading reviews, so I decided to treat the cancer info as if it were a troll, and block it.

There were positive factors. She was only forty-three, she was healthy, had never smoked, barely drank – and perhaps we had caught it in time. She had every hope of being one of those stories that people share to make others feel better.

Rach asked for more diazepam and I leapt up, marching towards the nurses' station as my trainers squeaked briskly on the vinyl floor tiles. I swung open a thin white curtain, behind which a nurse was making notes, and I requested some more drugs.

'I'm sorry, it's a little soon since her last tablet,' the nurse replied. 'We have to monitor . . .'

'She's just been told she's got fucking cancer. She's got two kids. Come on, give her the drugs,' I said in a voice that didn't belong to me. *Come on, give her the drugs.* I sounded utterly ludicrous. But I didn't care.

She looked at me sympathetically and I realised that I had just sworn at a nurse. 'I'm sorry I swore just now.'

'It's not easy,' she said sweetly. 'It's a difficult time for you all.'

She reached out to stroke the faux fur trim on my cardigan. I hadn't taken it off for the previous five days. My vigil uniform. I read once that Steve Jobs wore an identical outfit every day so that he didn't have to waste headspace on menial choices. Outliers and the terrified had a lot in common, it turned out; neither of us gave a shit about how we looked.

It was midnight. The nurses had waived the visiting hours for us but Rach looked shattered and needed to rest. We would hear the next steps tomorrow at 9.00am, once the consultant had the results of her various tests.

A calm resolve had descended on Rach by the time I prepared to leave. She used language such as 'not letting it defeat' her; 'beating it' and 'staying positive'.

I was waving goodbye, about to draw her bed curtain, when suddenly I found myself blurting out, 'Fucking cancer – fuck you, cancer. We're going to kick this fucking cunt in the arse!'

The elderly lady in the bed opposite stirred. Mum and Adam laughed.

Rach broke into a grin. 'Yeah, let's kick it in the arse!' She blew a kiss. And then she said softly, 'Night, C.'

29 December

I arrived early at the hospital today, perhaps for the first time in my life. Punctuality and I had never really had the best relationship. Jane and Jonathan had developed strategies to manage 'Emily time'. 'The movie starts at 7.30!' they would say, when it began at 8.00. But I needed to ingratiate myself with time now that it had decided to start making threats to my sister.

I stopped at the food court to pick up some satsumas for Rach and take a call from my godmother, Penny. She and the Phillips family, her husband John and three boys had been friends since our childhood. They acted as a comforting bridge between us and the dog-family world, their lively artsy domestic life similar to ours but underpinned by estate cars and promptly paid bills. *Bon viveurs* who knew when it was time to leave the party. Penny had walked this path before with her husband's cancer diagnosis, and was throwing her fixing skills at it all, calling her contacts at the Marsden hospital. Meanwhile Jane was researching specialist centres in LA. You gravitate towards life's decisive architects at times like this.

My stomach gurgled. I hadn't eaten a meal since yesterday morning. Food felt oddly decadent, somehow. The nervous hunger was a new addition to my recently formed gang of unexpected companions. It joined the wrecking ball in my stomach and our crazy new pal, insomnia.

Adam, Mum and I sat nervously around Rach's bedside, waiting for the consultant. I suggested to Rach that I record the conversation we were about to have on my phone, so that we could keep track of all the medical stuff. She nodded.

The consultant arrived. She had wiry hair and was dressed in a neat collared jumper and skirt. She looked like an Agatha Christie character – the one you never thought to suspect. I smiled at her warmly, as if charm might have the power to affect the outcome in some way.

'I feel we have a clear idea of where we are now,' she said to Rach. 'I'd like to understand what you understand.'

'Well, I'm just trying to deal with things, really,' Rach said calmly. 'In some ways it's a relief to know what's going on. Once you know . . .'

Rach went through the swift decline of the previous few weeks: exhaustion, feeling breathless when walking Giggle, going off her food and the endless fevers. The 'stubborn baby weight', which we now knew was a swollen abdomen related to the cancer. 'I just put it all down to having had a baby earlier this year.'

'Yes, yes I see.' The consultant nodded, absorbing the information, weighing it up like the boss who respectfully allows you to have your say, before delivering the outcome that has already been decided.

'Would now be a good time to tell you about the results?' she asked. 'Because the disease is in your liver, and there's quite a lot of disease in your liver. We need to try and control the activity of the cancer. Steroids are a very good—'

Rach interrupted her. 'Can I ask you something?' she said with a calm dignity. 'Would you say it was quite advanced?'

'What stage is it?' I demanded suddenly. I immediately regretted it, feeling I had overstepped the mark, crashed through the polite medical process with reckless indelicacy.

To my relief, Rach sanctioned the question.

'Yes, what stage?' she repeated evenly.

The consultant shifted her position, leaning forward and clasping her hands together gracefully.

'When disease has gone to your liver and we know it's come from somewhere else,' she paused, 'then the cancer is Stage Four.'

Stage Four. There was no Stage Five.

'Oh my God. That's bad, isn't it,' Rach said, shock spreading over her face. 'So the chances aren't good, are they?'

She looked to Adam, Mum and me for help. The wrecking ball exploded in my stomach.

Adam grasped her hand tightly and addressed the consultant with authority. 'Look, from our point of view, we just want you to be as aggressive as you can in treating this. There's no time to lose now. We can—'

'Stage Four, guys,' repeated Rach. 'That's awful.'

Adam continued. 'I really feel that we should go full-on with chemotherapy; she's young and we believe she can handle it—'

Rach cut through. 'What are my chances?'

'I'll try and answer all of your questions,' the consultant said in the patiently resigned tones of someone faced with a baying media scrum.

'Is there any hope?' asked Rach.

'There is hope that we can try and control the disease. But if you're asking me can we cure you . . .' She trailed off.

'How long do you think I have?'

'Again, that's difficult.'

'What about a liver transplant?' asked Adam.

'I'm afraid a liver transplant in your case would not be a feasible option.'

'So I'm going to die, basically,' said Rach. 'How long have I got?'

'We're going to control it,' said Mum.

'Is there any hope for surgery at all?' persisted Adam.

'How long has she got?' I said simply.

The consultant paused. 'Is that something you really want to hear today, Rachael?'

'Yes.' The word was so small. And yet so strangely apocalyptic.

'No doctor anywhere can predict this with certainty. But based on the rate of disease,' her voice softened, 'we think it will now be a matter of months.'

'I have a ten-year-old. And a baby. I can't leave them,' Rach said.

Adam fought back his tears, talking forcefully about treatment and transferring hospitals. My mother had disappeared behind a mask of shock and denial, producing print-outs from the internet and challenging the consultant with cancer-survival stories.

I went to the end of Rach's bed and curled up, placing my head on her feet. I just wanted to shut out the world and stay there, forever.

Rach was absorbing this with a grace that floored me. I had known exactly what she was thinking at every moment throughout our lives. But I didn't know how it felt to be told you wouldn't be here in a matter of months. How was she managing to not scream or collapse, how did she remember to say please when she just asked for a glass of water? There was no right way to respond to news like this. You react how you react. But I realised that my sister wanted us to wrap her in a calm blanket – the one in which she had always enveloped her own children.

I had sensed her wanting to shield Mimi from the burden of the diagnosis, to protect her from this trauma and keep her away from the hospital. The peaceful childhood Rach wanted for her, one that needed to differ greatly from ours, couldn't possibly accommodate this.

Rach asked me to get her some more diazepam. We've joked about me becoming her dealer; I've been doing a comedy Harlem accent to amuse her, every time I hand over the drugs. 'Daddy's got some sweet sugar for his girl!' But it felt wrong today.

As I headed out to the nurses' station I felt light-headed and nauseous. My ears started to ring. I stared down at my trainers and then suddenly my legs gave way. I connected with the cold hospital floor.

Two nurses rushed over. 'Her sister is in bed seven,' I heard one whisper by way of explanation.

'I'm fine, it's just lack of food,' I said. I didn't want Rach to know that I had collapsed. Noisy Em, making the moment about her, stealing focus.

They sat me down and brought me water and I attempted to wave the moment away with comedy, recalling an observation we made on the radio show once, that fainting wasn't a real 'thing', it was just attention-seeking.

One of the nurses smiled. 'Well, actually, it is very much "a thing,"' she said, explaining patiently that shock reduces blood flow to the brain.

I just wanted to go back to that place where we had laughed about fainting. Where the idea of being physically overwhelmed by news felt like a preposterous one.

The mood behind the curtain had changed by the time I got back. The 'Fuck cancer' battle cries of the night before had gone, replaced by disbelief.

Rach asked to see a priest, who was brought from the hospital chapel. He was informal and gentle and sympathetic, listening mainly, asking questions about her children and her life, talking about hope and the human spirit. She looked relieved.

I had always adopted my father's rational approach to faith. I couldn't understand how anyone could argue against science and logic. But those dinner-party assertions about the absurdity of belief in the afterlife now seemed ridiculous. Just as the medics had become responsible for fighting to keep her here, the priest seemed to offer her a way of coping with the moment when they had to admit defeat. A sense of something greater than merely ceasing to exist. It might not be my way, or my father's way, but who was I, who were any of us, with our complacent luxury of a future, to argue with her choice?

My dad arrived with his messenger bag slung over his body, his eyelashes wet with sorrow. He engaged the priest in a discussion about Matthew Arnold's poem about faith, 'Dover Beach', steering things into a more literary, philosophical terrain. The priest looked impressed by his knowledge and my father warmed to his approval.

I felt myself instinctively reacting with rage. *This is her moment. Her time to be the painting. You must be the frame now*, I wanted to scream. He took the full silent weight of my own guilt. It was less painful than dealing with mine. The feeling that I had spent my whole life trampling on Rach's kind, generous heart, blurting out unkind things. Dominating our shared space and leaving her no room to breathe. I wanted to reboot our history, take back every thoughtless remark I had ever made, every disapproving thing I had ever said. I wanted to atone for it all, and apologise.

But confessions are sometimes for ourselves, not for the people we confess to. So I decided to sit with the discomfort. Perhaps if I was helpful, pragmatic and useful enough, I could make it up to her.

30 December

I waited for my sister to shout, to scream at the injustice of it all. For the shock to subside and usher in anger. But that didn't happen. She stayed wrapped in peaceful introspection, 'her bubble', as she called it. 'I can shut out the rest of the world, and in a way it's easier for me, Em,' she said. 'My bubble protects me.'

I decided that I would take indefinite leave from the radio show and my magazine job when the Christmas break ended the following week, so that I could be by Rach's side every day. The solid defender on our dedicated team surrounding Rach. My godmother, Penny, called often and reframed our confusion with positive action, insisting that she would call her various contacts to get Rach swiftly transferred to the Royal Marsden in Chelsea. 'It's the best cancer hospital in the world. Rachael deserves the best,' she said decisively.

Rach asked me to get thank-you presents for the nurses. 'Just some little beauty products, freebies you have from the magazine, maybe?' She spent several hours laying out all the lipsticks and mascaras and body oils on the bed, and writing cards. 'This lipstick would suit Tiara's skin tone, don't you think? And this perfume is very her.' She rearranged the cosmetics endlessly. 'I like doing this, Em. I feel normal again, choosing presents.'

I told her that I would have to try to sneak them into their staff room. 'I think the NHS have jobsworth rules about accepting gifts. I don't want to be in the *Sun* tomorrow. "The Evil Face Of Cancer Drug Bribes!"'

'You know,' she said, placing mascaras and hand creams in

gift bags, 'I want you to help with Mimi's periods and get her Tampax. And you should take her to buy a bra. It's nice to have a woman in your life for things like that.'

She placed a bow on a bag.

It was the first time she had addressed the concept of not being here anymore. I sensed that she couldn't allow herself to dwell in that place for too long. 'When I'm gone' conversations were not ones she wanted to have. And sometimes, I allowed myself to think she would be one of those miracle stories who made it to the other side. The maverick outlier. Not like the others.

31 December

It was New Year's Eve. I was resting on the bed that Adam often used, in our makeshift hospital camp. His mother had moved in to their place to look after Mimi and Bertie. Adam and Rach were keen to normalise things for Mimi. This illness was obviously out of the ordinary but she didn't know the full implications.

Rach had constant fevers and was dependent on the relief of the cool fans and doses of medication. She would be starting her treatment at the Royal Marsden in a few days, which had lifted her spirits. It represented a positive new start, a place where dire prognosis was often turned round, where 'impossible' sometimes became 'maybe'.

The day before she'd told me she wanted to laugh and take her mind off things, so the previous night I'd stayed up until 4.00am, manically downloading every episode of her favourite TV programme, *Peep Show*. I threw in her other favourites, Alan

Partridge, an Alan Carr comedy special and Paul O' Grady's last tour. I rationalised that the more I downloaded, the more time she would have left. It was simply not possible for someone to be watching *Peep Show* one day and cease to exist the next.

I was immunised from the significance of New Year's Eve in our hospital bubble but it assaulted me when I wandered out to Sainsbury's to buy Rach some juice and fruit. A huddle of teenage girls were choosing flavoured vodka drinks and bags of Doritos, playing Rihanna on their phones, fizzing with anticipation over their plans. Couples came in clutching each other against the cold, selecting wine from the chilled cabinet to take to parties. I averted my eyes from them, aware that I was now a member of a shadowy sub-species, who had clambered into their jubilant seasonal world and was threatening to harsh their high with my foggy gloom.

My phone bleeped with what Rach called 'lazy-bastard texts' from old acquaintances – those serve-all, generalised New Year greetings, decorated with party poppers and champagne bottle emojis. 'Have the best one ever!' 'Here's to all you dream of in 2012!' 'Gonna be a good one!'

It was eerily quiet back on the ward. Pensioners were receiving dutiful visits from family members and a TV blared out the National Lottery draw in the visitors' room, watched by a lone man in a fleece and slippers. I returned to my safe place, resting my head on Rach's feet, and watched her as she slept, scanning for any sudden changes in her breathing. I wondered whether this was what it felt like to look after a newborn child. Constant panic blended with vigilant love. She had always looked after me, and now we had reversed our roles. If I just kept watching her, maybe she wouldn't leave.

2 January 2012

Rach went home. She was going to spend a few days there before she started her treatment at the Royal Marsden. Even though she was frail and wiped out, her face brightened when she re-entered the noisy domestic scene of dogs and children.

'Giggle was so excited to see me he's ACTUALLY pissed everywhere, Em!'

Giggle didn't seem to be especially adept at controlling his emotions. His eyes on stalks, he attached himself to her ankles, whining and following Rach around like a deranged groupie.

Adam installed Rach upstairs in their sunny attic bedroom overlooking the garden, where she could rest and build up her strength before chemo. She had been deluged with thoughtful gifts from friends: cashmere pyjamas, organic beauty products, magazines and paraffin-free scented candles. I arranged for my manicurist friend, David, to come and give her a pedicure. 'I think it's a pink day!' he announced, distracting her with tales of fashion runway dramas and high-maintenance clients. He waved away my attempts to settle the bill, insisting, 'It was an honour!'

I could see that Mimi was relieved to have Rach back home and normality restored. My mum brought Bertie upstairs to gurgle on the bed, and the nightmare of the hospital drama felt diminished. Rach sent out Facebook messages to all her friends. 'Sorry to sound like an Oscar winner but I need to thank these wonderful people!' she said with customary camp largesse. She carefully documented each offer of childcare and every bunch of flowers, refusing to let the cancer rob of her courtesy and grace.

3 January

The Rosses had offered to lay on a car and driver to take Rach to her first consultation at the Marsden. 'Look, it'll just be one less thing to worry about,' Jonathan said, downplaying it.

During painful times, people often end messages with the phrase 'If there's anything I can do . . .' It's a well-intentioned, socially decent offer that I myself had extended many times in the past. But it was only now that I understood the power of doing rather than asking.

Our friend Kaz brought round dishes of home-cooked lasagne for the whole family. Rach's college pal, Alice, booked a flight over from America, despite having just given birth. One of Rach's mum friends swept in to help out with Mimi and distract her with playdates. James, my primary school friend, was about to arrive on a plane from Washington. He had lost his mother to cancer and knew the implications of Rach's diagnosis.

I realised how much we are conditioned to tread around people who are in pain. We worry about causing offence, over-stepping the mark, intruding. But Rach was entering a country that had no time for such genteel reservations, and we were heading with her. No need to even ask. Just do.

A few months previously, Rach had managed to get tickets for the sold-out play *Jerusalem*. She had spent three days repeatedly refreshing the ticket site, to buy three seats. She'd planned to go with her friends Helen and Vicky but was simply not up to it now. I could fix this, I decided. I would not ask – I would do.

I spent the day calling my colleagues at the magazine, then the theatre manager, trying to swap the *Jerusalem* tickets for a date after her chemo had started. A matinee perhaps, when the West End would be less noisy and overwhelming.

4 January

'Em, I want to ask you something,' Rach said to me the day after my flurry of theatre-related phone calls. I was sitting on her bed, massaging her feet. My mum was pottering about downstairs with the girls. Adam had rushed up to Whole Foods to stock up on organic produce, urged by a friend whose wife managed to overcome a similarly ominous prognosis.

'I want you to go to *Jerusalem* in my place. I want you to see it for me. And tell me what it's like.'

'No, we can postpone the tickets, I've been making arrangements—'

'I want you to see it for me,' she said decisively.

I didn't want to address what I feared. That she suspected she might not get to see it. She would never have said that out loud; it was simply not her way. I wondered, with a creeping sense of shame, whether I would have been capable of such a generous act in her position. Wanting to gift your experience to others, for your pain to become their joy, despite the sheer injustice of life continuing without you.

'Of course! That's so sweet of you,' I told her.

'I want you to have a laugh with my friends. Go out and get pissed with them afterwards. Promise?'

'I solemnly promise we'll get pissed, Rach, yes.'

6 January

The black Mercedes that Jonathan had arranged to take us to and from Rach's appointment at the Marsden snaked out of Rach and Adam's street. A mile into the journey Rach needed to vomit.

The driver stared ahead without uttering a word, pulling up obediently outside a Sainsbury's as I raced in to get a carrier bag to use as a makeshift sick bowl.

'Sorry about this,' Rach apologised to the driver.

He nodded repeatedly, still stonily silent.

'Maybe-no-speak-ENGLISH?' my mother stage-whispered at me.

We continued through the traffic, Rach talking about the Marsden being the best place possible. The atmosphere in the car felt faintly optimistic, as if the word 'hope' had suddenly swung by for a visit.

We pulled up outside the hospital and Adam gently helped Rach out of the car.

The eerily mute driver suddenly leaned out of the car window to address me.

'Excuse me,' he whispered apologetically, waiting until the others were out of earshot. 'I hope I do not seem rude. I am told for this job not to say one word EVER to the passengers. They tell me peace and silence.'

We sat drinking coffee in the waiting room before Rach's

appointment. I told them about 'one word EVER', imagining Jonathan giving draconian instructions to the car company, which the driver seemed to have taken rather literally.

'I wondered why the poor bastard looked so terrified!' My mother laughed.

'How thoughtful of Jonathan. Everyone is being so kind,' said Rach.

Rach had never chosen to be the centre of the picture. She seemed almost baffled by the rush of deference being thrown her way. She had never felt entitled to lavish bouquets or solicitous drivers and people monitoring her every movement. So she accepted this blast of attention with a slightly stunned gratitude, an appreciative stranger in this new land.

We were ushered in to see her consultant, Dr Cunningham, who had a sympathetic, paternal manner. He confirmed that she had colon cancer, which had metastasised (I learned recently this means 'spread') to her liver. Notoriously, colon cancer could be hard to detect, which was why in Rach's case there had been no obvious signs until it had spread to other organs. Surgery on her liver at this late stage, he explained, with this type of cancer, was not an option. But he didn't dwell on this, instead suggesting ways of managing the disease. He told her that she needed to forget picking at raw diets and instead load up on calorie-rich foods. The priority now was to get her strong for chemotherapy. He focused on what he could do now, rather than worst outcomes.

We all headed home, diverting via the West End to drop me off at the theatre. It was the night of *Jerusalem*. I needed to say something to Rach. I wanted to pitch my tone right

– to keep it light and not treat the occasion with weighty solemnity. That was not how Rach dealt with things. It never was.

'Wish me luck. Those two will be stuck into the white wine already.' I smiled.

Helen and Vicky are the couple you hope will arrive first at a party. The ones who seize the karaoke mic, pull the elderly relative on to the dance floor and finally take you to an after-hours bar where you have to buzz three times and ask for someone called Spider.

'Well, I'm green with envy, dear!' my mother said, taking her cue from me. *I think this is the way to handle it*, her glance communicated.

But I realised suddenly that there was no need for this careful monitoring of language. Rach had acquired the unfettered honesty of someone focused purely on living now. Time spent on selecting the correct words to deliver in the appropriate way was time wasted.

'I want to hear all about it!' Rach said, as I climbed out of the car.

I felt strange standing outside the five-star billboards for the play. Guilty about stealing her experience. And panicked by her absence – as if we had fast-forwarded to a future that I didn't want to think about. But then Helen and Vicky arrived and covered me in cold-cheeked embraces, and laughter.

Our three seats were, as my mother would say, 'up in the bloody gods', and the stage was partially blocked by lighting equipment. Helen spotted an empty box and we snuck down there, dodging past ushers and giggling rebelliously. I was glad we had managed to come away with an anecdote that would make Rach laugh.

'How AMAZING was that?' said Vicky afterwards.

'I know,' Helen agreed. 'I really wanted to tell Rach, "You missed nothing! Fucking overrated. We fell asleep." Do you think she'll buy it if we tell her it was an absolute pile of shite?'

8 January

'Tell me about *Jerusalem*, Em.'

I decided she was unlikely to buy the 'absolute pile of shite' line, so opted for the truth.

We were at my mother's house in Muswell Hill for our postponed Christmas. Adam was bouncing Bertie on his knee; Giggle was pacing around, high on the scent of turkey, cynically working my mother's tendency to over-indulge his endless appetite.

My dad started talking about *Jerusalem*. I wasn't sure he had actually seen the play. But that was the kind of detail that rarely bothered him. 'An extraordinary performance. Mark Rylance is easily our greatest living stage actor,' he said grandly, letting out a large fart that no one acknowledged except Mimi, who gave an elated gasp.

Rach grinned at me. My mother was stirring the special gravy she always made from a yellowing Delia Smith newspaper cutting. The tree was buckling under the weight of the bizarre decorations she had kept since our childhood. We never had red baubles. Instead there was a blue Afro-wigged angel, a little photo Rach put in a tiny frame of me having a tantrum and a miniature African wood carving of a naked woman that our grandmother gave us one year.

It was hot and noisy in the small kitchen, with an orchestra of competing voices. Rach looked weary.

'Do you want to come and sit up here, Rach?' I suggested, and she nodded, slowly mounting the three steps up into my mum's living room area, cluttered with chipped bowls of potpourri, theatre prints and Mimi's drawings. She sat in the battered chesterfield chair gifted to my mother by Lynsey several years ago, which now had exploding innards held together by gaffer tape. 'That chair is SO our family,' Rach said once. 'Decaying decadence. You can hear it screaming, "How have I ended up in this weird place?"'

She glanced at the continuing discussion about Shakespeare in the kitchen. Comforted to have it in the background but wanting space from it sometimes. Just as it always was.

'You see, YOU get me,' she said, of the subtle rescue mission.

'We get each other,' I replied.

Mimi urged Rach to open her long-overdue Christmas presents. Rach took her time over it, partly because of her diminished energy but also because that was how she approached everything. With deliberation, rather than frenzied gorging.

She got to my gifts: a gold necklace, a cashmere top and the hairdresser vouchers for a cut and highlights.

I had started to panic about the hair vouchers the night before, wondering whether the escalating events of the previous week had rendered the present wildly inappropriate. 'You're about to have chemo and lose your hair, here's a tasteless reminder of the life you've left behind!' I considered removing the envelope with its silk bow from under the tree. And then decided that would be not be in keeping with the way Rach was dealing with this – wanting to stay positive, talking about the future.

'Thought it would be something to look forward to after . . . everything,' I said awkwardly as she opened it.

'Oh, Em,' she said quietly.

I felt sick. I had got it hopelessly wrong.

'Rach, I didn't want to upset you! It's for after the chemo, for when . . .'

'No!' she said. 'Don't be stupid. I'm crying because it's such a generous present.' She hugged me. 'It's so nice, that's all.'

I couldn't decide whether she was being honest. But it made me wonder how much this mantle of optimism she had fashioned was for all of us rather than her. I had no idea what was really going through her mind when 'the future' was mentioned.

11 January

A few days later, preparations for Bertie's first birthday got underway. Rach had decided to throw a little party at the house, and sent out Facebook invites to friends. She told them that if anyone had a cold or virus they would need to stay away as she was trying to protect her immune system.

'Weekends are busy for you all, don't worry if you can't make it!' she said. 'Turn up when you like.' She sounded like a working mum who understood the chaotic lives of other working mums. Rach had never been uptight about arrangements and was baffled when people responded angrily to altered plans or late arrivals. Her house style had always been 'No dramas, mate!' a phrase we picked up in Australia. It still was.

13 January

Two days before Bertie's party Rach was resting. She was trying to build up strength for the operation to have her chemo port, a small disc through which the drugs could be administered via a tube, inserted next week.

I was worried about her coping with a party. I suggested to Mum that we talk to Adam about keeping things more low-key.

'It's her daughter's first birthday, Em,' Mum said simply.

15 January

Rach put on a bright silk shirt and some eyeliner and lipstick for the party. She had lost a lot of weight and looked frail. Shock flashed briefly across her friends' faces before they embraced her. But she had thrown out the cancer narrative for today. She complimented someone on their skirt. 'Is that Zara? I'm so copying you, sorry!' She told a funny story about Mimi, and laughed with a friend about how all newborns look 'basically like Ross Kemp'.

Adam brought in the cake, with a giant pink iced number one, which had been organised by one of Rach's friends. ('Darling, is it just me or does the number one look more like a pound sign? You have to be SO careful with high-street bakers,' my mother whispered.) Rach posed with Bertie on her lap as Mimi blew out the candles for her.

On the way home in the car my mum told me how happy she was to see Rach surrounded by her friends, wrapped up in love and concern.

'Her friends have always been like an extended family for her. And she wants to share that with her girls . . .'

She trailed off, aware that we were heading into dangerous waters with the mention of things Rach wanted to cultivate in her daughters' lives.

'I really think she is going to beat this, you know,' she said, shifting swiftly into another gear. 'Rach is a fighter!'

I nodded silently.

16 January

I popped into my magazine office a few days later. Partly because I felt guilty about my long absence, which still had no end date in sight, but also to thank my boss, Eilidh, for being so understanding.

'Emily. Please. Don't even think about work,' Eilidh said. 'You need to be with your sister now. For however long . . .'

It was strange being thrust into the world of my immaculate fashion colleagues, with their glossy highlights, tailored blazers and spiky heels. I felt like a foreigner in this perfumed, elegant universe. The girls wrapped me in hugs but no one probed for information. 'Get out of fashion magazines, too many bitchy women!' a male friend once said. I now knew he was utterly wrong. There was an undeniable power in female friendships at times like this.

Alice, the Beauty Editor, offered to help source wigs for Rach and handed me a list of sensitive, specialist places – ones where we wouldn't encounter stag-night parties piling in to ask 'for twelve Austin Powers wigs. Lads on tour!'

Rach had told me she wanted the wig to be right so that she didn't frighten Mimi. 'I need to still look like her mummy. I don't want her to worry. Find me a good one, Em. And for fuck's sake, make sure it's not the sort of thing Matt Lucas wears in *Little Britain* when he's playing a woman.'

17 January

I met Mum at the wig shop in Notting Hill. There was an elderly lady with alopecia, browsing. The other customer was a woman wearing a headscarf who looked about Rach's age, her missing eyebrows and lashes telling their own story. I offered her a friendly smile. Before, I would have thought it best to discreetly avert my gaze.

'What about this?' my mum said, picking up a buttery blonde layered one with a fringe and ash highlights.

'No, a bit "newsreader going through marriage problems",' I said, lapsing into the waspish shopping shorthand Rach and I used.

I found a champagne-coloured shoulder-length one with flicked-out ends. 'This is the one,' I said. 'She can wear it with a scarf to hide the parting. Bad partings are the truth-tellers with wigs.'

My mum agreed. 'Oh, darling, you are so clever! This is perfect.' My mobile rang. It was Adam. I went outside to take the call. The cancer was spreading. He mentioned lymph nodes. And bones. He told me that Rach didn't want to burden my mum with this news. She worried Mum wouldn't cope. In just the same way she didn't want to worry her friends – or Mimi. He told me Rach wanted to keep it between the three of us. 'I understand,' I said, watching my mum through the window, engaging the shop assistants in laughter as she tried on unflattering hairpieces to amuse them.

'Who was that?' Mum asked as I entered the shop.

'Oh, just Adam checking in.' My breeziness was too forced. 'Shall we get—'

'Is everything okay, Em?'

'Yep, all fine.'

18 January

It had been three weeks since the Agatha Christie consultant broke the news. Rach didn't want to dwell on the cancer's ceaseless march upon her body. She urged all of us to get back to normal, accept invitations, start dipping back into work. She wanted me to go back to the radio show. 'Please, Em, I want everyone to be living their lives. It's depressing otherwise.'

I told Frank I was going to return to the show that weekend. 'Only if you're sure, Em,' he said, warily.

I had been popping back into the magazine office for the odd hour but had spent most of every day over the past fortnight keeping vigil in Rach's bedroom as she built up her strength for chemo. 'Hey, C,' I shouted as I raced up the stairs every morning. We gossiped about friends, pored over the endless gifts and teased Mum as she read out passages from a cancer survivor's story. 'Why do actors always read everything as if they're auditioning for *Macbeth*?' Rach giggled to me. I watched over her while she napped, counting the minutes until her eyes opened again.

20 January

Rach started chemo at the Marsden yesterday. But when Mum and I popped in today to see her after her second session, she was in a lot of pain. 'This is worse than childbirth,' she gasped, gripping the bed. But she somehow still managed to pass on the sighting of 'a really fit doctor' for me. I laughed to cover up the panic I felt. And because it was just so her.

Consultants paced in and out, asking her questions with a calm professionalism.

Mum and I retreated to the waiting room while they investigated further. Adam explained a few hours later that they would be keeping her in overnight. He would call to let us know how she was getting on.

'She's in the best place, at least,' I said to Mum as we headed home. 'Thank fuck for that hospital. I'm sure her body's just trying to deal with the chemo. It's basically poison,' I pointed out, with that slightly know-it-all tone of someone who's overheard a few doctors talking and decided they are now a medical expert.

The other day, during one of our bedside chats at home, Rach had asked me to look into a big family holiday for all of us – her, Adam and the girls, me and Mum. 'Somewhere hot and lovely,' she'd said. 'Soon, Em.' So I decided to spend the evening researching destinations.

I had always sensed she felt slightly caught between two worlds – her past with us and the new one she built for herself.

Our family story was too all-consuming to recede politely into the background. But now, she was simply able to ask for what she wanted: to bring those worlds together.

I started to Google short-haul winter-sun holidays. Seeing the sparkling pools and 'available now!' notices filled me with hope. 'The only family holiday we ever had was the shit sandwich to tell us they were divorcing,' Rach once said. I was going to put this right.

My phone rang.

'Em?'

It was Adam.

'They've taken her to the intensive care unit,' he said. 'She's in a bad way. They think . . . it'd be a good thing to gather at her bedside now.'

Intensive care. Bad way. The words didn't make sense. It was too soon.

'I'll call Mum. We're on our way.'

Mum sounded merry when she picked up. Her spirits had been lifted by Prosecco and the company of her old actor friend, Hugh Quarshie, who had popped in to see her. 'Hugh's here! He was just talking about that time—'

'Mum, Adam called. Rach has been taken to intensive care. She's in a bad way.'

She gasped. And then went silent.

It was Hugh's voice I heard next. 'Emily, I'll drive you. We'll see you in ten. Hang on in there,' he said in his deep resonant voice.

I felt almost high on the car journey to the hospital – strung out on shock. My mother sat in the front, cloaked in silence.

Bright optimism had carried her through her entire life but it was a currency rendered obsolete now. I thought of her parking on yellow lines outside Harrods as she unleashed her Churchillian battle cry, 'The Dean luck will be on our side, girls!' She couldn't call on that anymore.

Hugh kept up a soft stream of conversation. It was a relief to have his robust presence buffering our raw fear. A family friend invested in the enormity of our journey but not sprawling, bewildered in the centre of it. He played a surgeon in the BBC medical drama *Holby City* and mentioned the potential confusion when he entered a hospital, as people struggled to separate life from drama. It was a conversational ramp I clung to, one that bridged the world of our childhood thespian anecdotes and the realm Rach now inhabited.

'We're here,' Hugh said.

The doors swung open to take us into the hushed womb of the intensive care unit with its whispered conversations and hulking equipment blinking out numbers. The consultant gathered us into a small family room to talk about Rach's condition. The medical team referred to things like 'systemic failure', 'organs struggling', 'morphine' and 'monitoring her constantly'. The words landed with thuds.

I looked through the window of the room where Rach was lying. Her eyes were half closed and she was hooked up to all sorts of apparatus, her hair piled up in its signature messy half-ponytail.

'Can I see her?' I asked a nurse, who led me over to hand-sanitiser and thin plastic gowns and aprons, the strangely futuristic uniform that marked out the visitors in this unit.

I drew up a chair to her bed. 'Hey, Rach,' I said, stroking her hand.

She nodded towards a little bowl with a wet sponge on a stick. I lifted it up to her lips to moisten them. Her eyes looked different. I wasn't sure whether it was the medication or shock. *How the fuck has this happened in three and a half weeks?* her expression seemed to say. I stroked her hair in place of answers.

There was a lot I wanted to tell her. I wanted to thank her for making me feel safe and loved. For navigating the choppy seas of our childhood, and throwing sunshine and laughter on dark moments. I wanted her to know that the way she lived her life – with compassion and kindness – was the right way. I wanted to tell her how proud I was of the values she was instilling in her girls, teaching them to be considerate and kind. Guiding them towards a life where they focused on their minds rather than their beauty. I wanted her to know that when she refused to let me take Mimi to see a movie called *27 Dresses* about a marriage-fixated bridesmaid, calling it 'brain-washing shit', she was right. And that when she told Mimi never to use words like 'fat' as an insult, and I told her to 'lighten up', I was wrong. I wanted her to know that even though she isn't perfect – sometimes guilty of wanting to please too much, often prone to obsessing over past slights, occasionally too frightened of confrontation to demand what she is due – she always strove to be better.

Most of all I just wanted to tell her that I had never loved anybody as much as I loved her.

But I didn't. Because it was her ending, not mine. It didn't feel right to impose a sense of closure on her life with some grand speech. The truth was, I had no idea how to handle this. My only experience of talking to the dying had come via movies, where vows are made, forgiveness is sought and life is brought to a neat conclusion. I didn't know how to say goodbye to my sister.

So I decided to just tell her how I was feeling right now.

'I want you to know . . . that I really love you. You make me a better person – you make everyone a better person. I'm so lucky to have you as my sister. You're basically my world, Rach. You always have been.'

She looked up and squeezed my hand.

A nurse padded into the room. 'How are we doing?' she asked, and our moment of heightened intimacy receded into a glow, like candlelight flickering but not quite going out.

Back in the waiting room, I rested my head on my mother's lap. She stared ahead, in silence, stroking my hair as we retreated into the roles of child and parent. It felt easier than being two frightened adults.

'She'll beat this, I know she will,' my mother said firmly, in a tone that said she couldn't entertain any other outcome.

The clock ticked towards 2.00am. I walked out to glance through the glass at Rach as she slept, watched over by Adam. We all had our own story with Rach and there was an unspoken respect for that between us, so I resisted interrupting his intimate moment.

The critical-care sister approached and patted my shoulder. 'It's up to you, but don't feel you can't go home and get some sleep,' she said. 'You need to look after yourselves.'

'But what if . . .' I trailed off.

'We'll call you if there are any changes. We're monitoring her every minute.'

We gathered up our things. I glanced over at Rach's handbag and her Top Shop leopard-print jacket, slung over the back of a chair. Taunting us, as if she had thrown it casually off her shoulders and was about to return to the room, fizzing with energy and anecdotes.

'Miracles happen all the time,' said my mum defiantly, in the cab home.

I nodded reluctantly. I wanted her to adjust the sails for what was coming. I felt as helpless as someone watching a thriller, yelling at the protagonist to flee from the house into the dark forest because the ambush hiding in the basement was worse. *Prepare yourself*, I wanted to scream. Be the sage adult. The keeper of uncomfortable truths. That way I can be the scared child. I felt the absence of Rach, suddenly. Our world simply didn't work without her in it.

21 January

'How are we faring this morning?' asked one of the consultants as he popped his head round the door into the waiting room. He came in, his lilac shirtsleeves neatly rolled up, lanyard dangling from his neck. His presence was distinguished but friendly, a headmaster temporarily burying his authority at the school fete. He joked about the quality of the vending machine coffee before expertly shifting gears into discussion of Rach's condition, telling me that they were doing their best to control her pain.

'Thank you for looking after her,' I said. 'Everyone is lovely in this unit. So kind. It's like a little cocoon.'

'Oh, that's nice to hear. It's funny; people always talk about living in the moment, don't they? But they rarely do.' He smiled. 'I think this is probably one of the only places where that really does happen every day.'

He was right. Not once had anyone brought up the future or even the following day. Instead, people talked always in the present tense. 'We are trying.' 'We are monitoring.' His remark stayed behind after he had gently closed the door. What happened yesterday, what might happen tomorrow, was never mentioned here. It was a little haven of now.

I put on my plastic apron and gloves and entered Rach's room. The nursing team had told us that earlier on, she seemed to be indicating that she wanted to see a priest. 'I think she'd like that,' I agreed, remembering how comforted she had been by the friendly, informal hospital chaplain who chatted to her after her diagnosis.

The elderly man who arrived half an hour later seemed keen to get straight to business. 'Weekends are busy,' he said, hurriedly placing a silk stole around his neck. As he recited long passages from the Bible in sombre, ceremonial tones my stomach lurched. This archaic language and high formality were all off. I'd really booked the wrong person for this gig. 'Awfully sorry, but this is not the religion we were after!' I wanted to say diplomatically. 'We were looking for something a bit lighter. Tad more spiritual and personal, perhaps?' Our intimate vigil space felt pierced with oppressive symbolism and finality.

I exchanged worried glances with my mother, who offered

me a camp grimace, the kind she reserved for hopelessly miscast actors.

'Well, *SHE* was a bit Fire and Brimstone, dear,' she said when he was gone, opting for the female pronoun, as if he were a drag queen.

It was an irreverent habit picked up from her gay friends in the theatre who liked to call Sir Ian McKellen Serena McKellen. She was doing, of course, what we had always done – alchemising disastrous moments into anecdotal light relief. And it was exactly how Rach would have handled it. But I was struggling to lapse into that familiar style over this incident. I should have thought ahead, done research, made a better booking.

It's funny how you can find yourself focusing on things like the wrong tone by someone's bedside when you're losing them. Art directing someone's final days, planning the perfect end. It feels easier, perhaps, than confronting the thing you can't face.

I talked to Jane when I got home that night at 1 a.m. She managed to bury her own shock to wrap me in support. My phone had filled up with messages from people wanting updates, offering to help and visit. I hadn't shared the true extent of Rach's situation with most people, respecting her wishes. But Penny had grasped exactly how things stood. When I spoke to her she said, with pragmatic compassion, 'I think, my Em, we are going to have to prepare for a swift and pain-less exit for our darling girl.' It was a relief to hear those words. 'Swift exit.' I was the child briefly on the receiving end of difficult truths, rather than the adult reluctantly delivering them.

Some of my friends had deduced that things were hurtling towards a conclusion we hadn't foreseen. They listened as I cried, reassuring me that a long, drawn-out illness might have given us time to adjust but would have been tougher on her.

'You know what? Either way it's shit, Em, it just is,' said one friend.

There was an inescapable honesty in this. The right type of priest, the right goodbyes, the right length of time between knowing someone was going and watching them go – perhaps there were no good or bad endings. There were just endings.

22 January

We were sitting by Rach's bedside, chatting in the style that we had fallen into over the previous thirty-six hours. One that protected her from discussions of the future and the world outside and just cradled her in the gentle hum of family exchanges. She was increasingly less responsive, sometimes lifting her head or gesturing. But the medical team told us she would hear everything we said. I once read an article about how hearing is considered to be one of the last senses to go. What did she want to hear? It was a question to which I would never know the answer. But perhaps anyone would just want to feel loved.

I scanned Rach's face for a flash of approval. She often responded to things that made her smile. Overheard conversations between nurses, descriptions of eccentric visitors in the canteen, scandalous updates about a friend's love life. Rach had always been obsessed with the tiny details of human interaction.

She would stay on a bus past her stop just to hear the end of an intriguing conversation.

'Tell Rach about the doctor, Em!' my mother suggested.

I retold the moment, from last night, when I was describing a consultant as 'the really hot one, a bit like a *GQ* model' only to discover that he was standing right behind me.

Rach looked up, intrigued. I'd made a dick of myself and that was anecdote touchdown for her.

The consultant/*GQ* model took it well, I told her. 'It's okay, worse things happen,' he had said, with a smile. Perhaps saying 'worse things happen' in an intensive care unit had been a bold moment of gallows humour on his part. Or maybe just a poorly chosen phrase he was also now reliving with horror. But I was grateful to him for gifting us this pocket of light relief. And he did *really* look like a *GQ* model.

Adam started to talk about the girls, recalling one of Mimi's 'kids say the funniest things' moments, when Rach suddenly reached out and grasped both our hands with a firmness that surprised me. Mustering strength from somewhere, her face set in concentrated resolve, she lifted my hand and Adam's up to be joined above her head. A gesture of unity. About the future, and her girls. She enveloped Adam in an embrace before falling back into the bed, exhausted.

I sat in the waiting room afterwards wondering whether it was her way of saying goodbye. Did people know that they were nearing the end? Was that some sort of ceremony of closure? When would it happen? Tomorrow? And then I shut the thought down. I'd forgotten the first rule of the intensive care unit – you never talk about tomorrow.

23 January

Adam and I were in the cab, on our daily journey to the Marsden. Rain dribbled down the windows as the cream villas of Regent's Park hulked into view. Commuters navigated the wet pavements, speaking into phones, preparing for the week. Was it Monday? I'd begun to lose track of the days, out of sync with the rest of the world and their hurried flat-white orders, all those infinitesimal decisions that build a twenty-four-hour period. It was hard to remember when those hundreds of daily flickering thoughts filled my head, like tea lights, before they were extinguished by the furnace blast of fear. I envied those people now.

The driver had Magic FM turned up loud, the familiar accompaniment to every cab ride in London. I wondered whether the drivers had held a meeting and collectively decided it provided the best all-purpose playlist – soothing enough for the broken-hearted and mainstream enough for the ride with a work superior, where you don't really want the songs to stray into territory like *'I'm a boss you a worker bitch.'*

'Wishing I was Lucky' by Wet Wet Wet suddenly filled the car. I was transported back to the little two-up two-down we lived in with Mum after our family imploded. Rach was the custodian of the precious *Top of The Pops* video on which we had recorded our favourites. It had *'Rach and Em's music – do not wipe!!'* scrawled across it in felt tip. 'Rach, get the tape out!' I used to yell and she would tolerantly indulge my fondness for Wet Wet Wet's frothy blue-eyed soul, which sat awkwardly next to her archive of Morrissey's reluctant outings on the same show.

The cheesy Eighties synths built into the chorus and I thought about what Rach would say if she were here. "Wishing I Was Lucky"? That's our relationship-defining song? Fucking hell.'

The medical team was gathered in the waiting room when we arrived, lined up formally as if awaiting a visit from wealthy benefactors. They greeted us with the deference of those charged with delivering difficult news.

My mum sat down with an expression of disbelief etched on her face. She was facing the moment she had promised herself wouldn't come. And then it did.

They told us that that Rach probably wouldn't last the day.

I fell into Adam's arms as we slowly absorbed the news that was lurking around the corner, waiting to strike. We tried to restore some semblance of calm as we prepared to enter Rach's room.

My mum's face was a mask of shock. 'I still believe she will get through this,' she said, almost angrily.

'We have to listen to the medical team. They've told us, Mum. Rach is going to die today.'

It came out all wrong. Cruel, unforgiving, brutal. The force of my tone was propelled by a knot tightening in frustration at our wildly differing approaches to this disaster. I was the adult finally snapping at a child when they repeatedly do what they were warned against. I knew why my words had landed so heavily. The detached, professional opinions of the consultants were one thing – but to hear the truth from me, so unadorned, clearly felt like a profound betrayal.

She looked at me with fury and confusion. 'I am not going to write her off. I am not like you. I have to believe,' she snapped.

'I don't know what to say to you anymore,' I sighed.

I left the room, marching angrily through the doors into the ladies' loos, and sat down on the cubicle floor. Stung by the suggestion that I'd written my sister off. Our exchange was prompted by fear – that we were losing her, that we were helpless to do anything about it. And we were fighting for ownership of her. Perhaps we always had been. But this conflict was crass here, today. Rach always said, 'Never fall out at Christmas – it's a bit Noel and Liam Gallagher.' And I figured we had to assume she would extend that rule to an intensive care unit.

'I'm sorry, Mum,' I told her, re-entering the room, soothed by time out and canteen tea, that comforting all-purpose solution in soap operas that actually holds some truth. 'I just want you to be prepared.'

'I know, I know. I'm sorry too, darling,' she said, holding out her arms, and I nuzzled my head into her neck and the woody amber scent of my childhood. But her eyes were glassy with refusal to really take in what was happening.

I called my father. He hadn't been part of our vigil over the last few days, something he accepted with good-natured grace, aware that his role in our lives had been too erratic to now warrant a place in the heart of it. I'd called him with updates about Rach and he had spoken eloquently about our collective pain. His sadness never dissolved into an entire loss of composure. Perhaps his philosophical outlook made him resigned to the tragedies of human experience. But he was still a father, about to lose his daughter.

The night before, I mentioned to him that I'd spotted a painting of Baroness Burdett Coutts in the Marsden. She was the Victorian philanthropist who financed the hospital. She also built Holly Village, and this odd coincidence brought back memories of that brief period in our childhood when we had something that felt like a home. 'How fascinating,' he had said, suddenly reaching for a TS Eliot quote to capture the symbolism of life's circle.

'As Tom said in the *Four Quartets*, "In my beginning is my end . . ."'

'Yeah. Keep it light, Dad.'

He chuckled. It was the standard Morecambe and Wise comedy dynamic we had always employed – him as slightly pompous highbrow, me as sceptical lowbrow, shooting him down.

I met him today at the intensive-care unit doors, messenger bag, as always, slung across his chest. He was holding a copy of *The Times* and raising a crumpled moist tissue to his eyes. I showed him to the area where the transparent gloves and aprons were kept and prepared him for the atmosphere on the other side of the glass.

'We mainly just talk quietly to comfort her, Dad. I'm not sure how much of it she takes in now. But . . . nothing heavy.' It was my way of saying 'don't start quoting passages from *Hamlet*.' And he nodded, self-aware enough to know that his ornate rhetoric might not sit comfortably here.

His face was a complicated blend of affection and agony as

he stood over the bed where Rach lay, breathing slowly underneath the paraphernalia of survival.

'Hey there, Wodge,' he whispered, using her childhood moniker, based, like so many, on a toddler's struggle to master their own name.

He joined us in our peaceful low hum of chat, and then suddenly started telling my mum about a David Hockney exhibition he had seen recently.

'I found Hockney's landscapes sensational – yes they're fundamentally less elegant . . .' He continued, talking about the Californian golden age and Hockney's graphic strengths.

I looked at my mum, in panic. Oh Christ. It was all getting a little late-night-arts-review. Not really final hours around a deathbed.

'It's on until April,' he said. The words floated in the air. I didn't want April mentioned. Exhibitions that would still be here when Rach wasn't.

It was my fault. I had forgotten to tell him the first rule: we don't talk about tomorrow in the intensive care unit.

I gave my mother a despairing glance.

'Darling, I think Em would prefer not to dwell on the Hockney, maybe?' she said.

'Yes, yes of course.' He shook his head at his own lapse in judgment. 'You're absolutely right.'

Every slightly outré remark my father had ever made had seen the three of us scurrying to cover it, leaping in like disaster-response units, trying to restore the social norm. There were only two of us now to share that workload. Thank God my mum had covered my shift this time.

Rach slept on peacefully, unaware of the complex pre-death dynamics taking place beside her.

I glanced at the clock, my new enemy. Willing it to stop.

'The Hockney thing, Dad,' I said when we left the room so that the nurses could make Rach comfortable. 'It's just . . . she loved Hockney. And I hate that she won't get to see it.'

He offered a hug. It wasn't something he and I did that often. Expansive affectionate gestures always belonged to my mother's arena. He tapped his hand repeatedly on my back, in that resolute way of someone raised by nannies in the 1930s, who learned about feelings from literature. 'Dad, you're so un-gesturing,' I once complained after some stiff hand-tapping on a childhood birthday. 'I think,' he said, laughing, 'the word you are perhaps searching for is "undemonstrative", Emmy.' But the stoical rhythm was strangely reassuring today, anchoring me in the past.

It was a couple of hours later when one of the nurses said, 'We thought maybe now would be a good time to move Rachael next door. If you would like.'

I knew what this meant.

The medical team had agreed we would let her slip into death peacefully in a smaller room, a quieter, less clinical environment where she would be liberated from all the machines.

My mum took one of the many bunches of flowers that had been sent and placed them in a vase. I found a patterned scarf in Rach's bag and laid it on the foot of the bed. The ward sister found a candle for us to light.

The nurses opened the door for us. Her blonde hair was escaping from a hair elastic in the way it tended to when she greeted you at the house, Bertie on hip, mug of tea in hand, Giggle panting at her heels. She looked more like herself again, free from all the apparatus. As if she were just making the most of the brief bliss of a lie-in, before the family noise erupted.

We sat silently and watched her breathing. I focused on the familiar curve of her mouth. 'How come Rach got the blue eyes AND the big lips,' I used to complain. Those 'great brows' that she always resisted over-plucking, calling it 'a fast route to *Coronation Street*-pensioner.' Her face was more familiar than my own, a monument to everything that reminded me of safety. It was home. As comforting and soothing as the smell of baby lotion or antique books or the sight of motorway signs on the journey back from Heathrow. I just needed her to hang on a little longer. We needed more time.

She exhaled slow, familiar breaths. The ones I used to hear when we shared a bedroom in Holly Village, when Rach's ability to switch off her active mind meant she always slipped off to sleep first. The ones that annoyed me when she dozed off during *Dirty Rotten Scoundrels* and I yelled, 'Rach, what was the point of even renting this video? Wake up!' The ones we have been listening to in her bedroom over the last few weeks as she encouraged us to carry on talking to her. 'I'm just resting my eyes for a bit.'

And then suddenly, they stopped.

'Rach?' I said. 'Has she gone?'

Mum called for the nurse.

The nurse came in, took Rach's pulse and said softly, 'Rachael's left us now.'

I was glad she had said 'left us'. It made it sound as if it was her decision to finally leave, rather than a life that was stolen.

Adam and I cried on each other's shoulders. My mother fell into my father's arms, united in the shared loss of a child.

'The best one has gone,' my father wailed suddenly to my mother. 'She was the apple of our eye.'

I was stung by those words, even if they were just Alzheimer's robbing him of self-censorship. But I believed them to be true. She was the best one. It felt like a hideous miscarriage of justice, as if someone had messed up our family narrative. The fast-living, stability-avoidant loner is clearly the character who should have burnt out mid-way, while the responsible, maternal heroine makes it through to the uplifting conclusion. Fewer lives would have taken a direct hit if it had been me; the collateral damage would have been less devastating. She had a more fundamental right to a future than me.

'He didn't mean that, Em,' Adam said quickly, seeing my face. 'Don't be upset. He's in shock.'

But my father had spoken the truth. And the truth is harder to recover from than a lie. Rach didn't live the kind of life that deserved to burn out swiftly and dramatically. She was entitled to a life of quiet old age and reflection.

The nurses asked if we would like to say our goodbyes individually. I headed in for my last moment with Rach.

I kissed her forehead. She belonged to another world now, not mine. It was almost my sister, but not quite. It was as if someone had made a very good Madame Tussauds waxwork of her, one which followed to the letter every single physical aspect of her face, but they had forgotten to add her essence.

I felt oddly peaceful sitting next to her. She would always be my home. Death couldn't change that.

The nurse offered to cut off some locks of her hair. 'It's a nice keepsake. For her girls, too,' she said sweetly. She organised the hair into bags. The locks curled up neatly like question marks. Pale golden strands that should have been hanging over glasses of Prosecco in family gastropubs, or whipped up by a sudden breeze on walks with the dog. They didn't belong in pharmaceutical polythene bags, in a room full of graphite-coloured machines.

'Take this, darling,' Mum said, and handed me Rach's coat. 'I think she'd have liked you to have it.'

It was the leopard-print Top Shop swing jacket Rach wore into hospital. She must have worn it only a handful of times. I put it on and enveloped myself in her smell. There was a Starbucks receipt in the pocket and an old hair bobble. Fragments of an ordinary day.

We headed in silent assent over to the tiny pub opposite the Marsden. I'm not sure why. To give the sudden brutality of loss some sense of occasion. Perhaps we wanted to prolong our proximity to her. It felt overwhelming in there after the antiseptic coolness of the intensive care unit. Doctors boomed to each other over pints as they discussed recently finished shifts. Glasses were thrown into the dishwasher, ice shovels burrowed into a steel chest, a cash drawer was slammed shut. We raised glasses of red wine in a toast to Rach – it felt the thing to do, to mark her existence with some vague ceremony.

The cab took us all back to north London. I didn't know what happened now. How this worked. Fear keeps you moving forward, endlessly on high alert. Grief seemed far more vast and complicated. But I didn't say any of this. Especially when I thought of Adam having to break the news to Mimi that her mother was not coming back. A conversation none of us could have imagined having, four weeks ago. My mum and I offered to come with him but I understood why he wanted to tell her quietly, by himself.

'Are you sure you don't want to come back to mine, darling?' my mum asked as we pulled up outside my house.

'No, I'll be fine. But call if you need me, Mum,' I said. 'Love you.'

And then I let myself into my flat, lay down on the kitchen floor and stayed there for a few hours. It was cold and the laminate flooring felt hard against my cheek.

I knew what Rach would have said if she'd appeared outside my door now.

'Em, what are you doing, you freak?'

And then we would have laughed.

30 January

I asked my colleagues to send me over a dress to wear for the funeral. We regularly borrowed sample clothes for magazine shoots and occasionally designers lent us outfits for big events. I decided that events don't get much bigger than burying my sister. I wanted a costume for the day, to be handed in afterwards along with my composure, not left hanging in my wardrobe as a daily reminder. But mainly, I knew she'd never forgive me for not sending her off in style.

'Dark or a colour, darling?' texted the fashion assistant.

'I want to wear black. I really appreciate this.'

'It's a privilege. You have to look the BEST for your darling sis xx'

Adam and I went to meet Bryce, the reverend who was going to be conducting the service. He was surprisingly young and handsome, with the hint of a blond hipster beard and two toddlers climbing all over the shabby vicarage furniture. It seemed right to have someone like him overseeing Rach's funeral, a parent at the same stage of life, suffering through Disney films while nursing a hangover after a friend's boisterous fortieth birthday party.

We settled on his sofa and he asked about Rach. His face briefly crinkled up when we mentioned Mimi and Bertie but he regained his composure and told us about a service he did recently for a father of a similar age who'd had a fatal motorbike accident.

'How are your parents coping?' he asked me.

'It's hard for them,' I said.

I didn't tell him about Mum and me snapping at each other in the funeral directors over the choice of casket, flowers and urn. About the tussle over whether to use the King James version of Corinthians, which refers to charity, or the newer version, which refers to love.

'The charity version's four hundred years old!' I said.

'I want the King James version for my daughter's funeral,' my mum replied, her voice firm.

We were fighting over irrelevancies. The funeral director diplomatically pretended not to notice. She'd clearly seen all this before. Grief churning up all sorts of strange emotions, people projecting the stress of loss onto obsessions over font size and hymns and who goes in which car.

We left the funeral directors and walked down the hill to see Adam and the girls. My mother said she'd arranged for us to visit some family friends for lunch the following day.

'I don't know if I'm up to it, Mum,' I replied. 'I think I want to spend some time alone.'

Which was true. But suddenly I also felt engulfed by her need to blend our loss into one, desperate to separate my mourning out from hers. The regular social arrangements she made with her vast circle of friends, which we were always expected to attend, felt suffocating without Rach. I knew that saying no marked a turning point in our relationship. It was a rejection of the way we'd always done things, the travelling triumvirate who would put on a great show, even now.

My mother stopped walking. 'It's all about you. What about me? Us? What about doing things as a family! I've lost my bloody daughter, Em.' I began to run. Not a jog. More like someone possessed. I raced past groups of schoolchildren, forcing them to disperse, nearly collided with a group of mums with buggies and dodged the workmen unloading scaffolding, who laughed at me. I ran until I arrived at Adam's, breathless and sweating.

My mother got there fifteen minutes later and we pretended that the dramatic tussle of wills had never happened. As if we had mutually realised that, as with affairs on location or bridal hissy fits, we were simply victims of context.

No one warns you that grief isn't just about crying into each other's arms – that you've lifted up a rock and you can't control what will begin to emerge. The entire infrastructure of our lives had disappeared along with Rach. I was reminded of something Frank once said about dynamics changing forever after you've had an epic row with someone. That it can be like two continents seismically separating. But that sometimes those new borders make a better world. I really hoped he was right. I'd completely buggered my ankle during that run.

9 February 2012

I was lying in bed talking to Rach on the morning of her funeral. It was a secret habit I'd been indulging in a lot over the fortnight since she died. I hadn't told people about our 'chats' because if someone told me that, I would think they'd lost it. And besides, it all felt a bit Miss Havisham, holding on to a relationship that had ceased to exist. Actually, it was worse. At least she had the dignity of a Gothic pile to waft around in. But there were things only Rach would get – and as Jane reminded me, 'She is still your sister. And you are still her sister.'

Sometimes I called her mobile, just to hear her voice saying 'leave a message, byeee.' It was a call into the void. I wanted the temporary relief of connection but I got a flood of fresh hurt when I was met with silence. And a side order of crazy to accompany my main course of loss. Later, a long time after she died, I would make one of my furtive calls to her and be hit with the message 'this number is no longer available', like the advice of a tough-love friend suggesting it was really time I 'moved on'.

People had reached out endlessly, with cards, emails, gifts and texts, small gestures of compassion that acted like shots of medication. My friend James Gilbey sent a note saying 'You need these' nestling inside a giant box of cupcakes. The house filled up with huge bouquets, four-page letters and a card that read 'No words – just love.' My friends had come into their own. Jane was pragmatic and kind, Frank signed off his texts with 'from an old man who cares about you very much.' When I apologised to Gareth, my old radio show pal, for crying down the phone, he said simply, 'Emily, your sister died.' Polly was a permanent presence, my former *Sunday Times* colleague Tony Chambers checked in constantly and Penny and her family swept in to help with the practicalities I couldn't face.

I chatted to my friend David about my dad's 'the best one has gone' remark, which had lingered in my mind. His view of it was lighter and more rational than mine. 'I honestly think he was just reaching for the sort of dramatic language King Lear would use – it's just very your dad,' David said. 'Please don't take it too seriously.' I managed a laugh when he told me this, imagining Rach rolling her eyes and coming to the same conclusion.

But there were times when grief swaddled me in disconnection and I felt like someone playing at being human, unable to fully engage in everyday life. I called these periods my kitchen-floor parties, in honour of the night after Rach died. I would curl up in a ball and just cry, letting the calls and texts go to voicemail until they stopped.

I was starting to realise there is a curious honeymoon period in the initial stages of mourning when everyone treats you with the same friendly indulgence extended to the celebrity. It's a land where turning up late, forgetting to respond to messages and having emotional outbursts is patiently tolerated. 'You have to make the most of that time,' I was warned, 'because people forget quickly, they move on. But you don't.'

I took the black dress off the hanger. It was a tiny sample size that would normally have seen me struggling to wrench my bum past its zip, but I rattled around in it today. The poster girl for the 'bereavement weight-loss plan'!

Mum and Dad arrived to pick me up. He was in his best suit and tie, smelling of toothpaste. She had painted over her grief with blusher, and her hair bore the kink of freshly removed rollers. We made the journey through the frost-covered streets to Adam and Rach's house where we were met with the welcome distraction of domestic noise. Giggle leapt up at us, barking wildly at the sudden influx of additional family members. My dad got on all fours to woof as he raced around and we all smiled at Giggle's antics. He served as a handy focus puller, the thing to talk about when you didn't want to talk about the big thing.

Mimi seemed quietly apprehensive. The other night when I was plaiting her hair I had said to her, 'It will be Mummy's day, when we celebrate how much we love her.'

She had written something for the order of service. My friend, Tony, designed the booklet for us. He noticed something we'd missed. 'It looks great,' he said over email. 'But it's quite formal. Might be nice to have something a bit more . . . Rach. That the girls can be part of, maybe?' I replied saying, 'Only a Scouser could get away with giving you a review of a funeral's order of service. You are absolutely right btw xx'

So now Mimi's note had been reprinted on the back page. It was written in lilac pen inside a red felt-tip heart with hundreds of kisses. She had included a photo of her cuddling Bertie, who was grinning from inside her inflatable swimming ring on their summer holiday last year.

Thank you for being such a great mum. You were such an amazing person. We love you and we will never ever forget you! We will miss you so much. You will always be our hero and we will always look up to you and love you! XXXXXXXX

It was beautiful.

I was clutching the print-out of my tribute to Rach, which I'd read out endlessly to myself in an attempt to crush the words into indifference. I found this surprisingly useful tip on a forum after searching 'how to get through a funeral speech'. I decided not to take the advice from one contributor in Alabama who suggested, 'Just get loaded, man.'

The funeral cars arrived. I caught a glimpse of Rach's wicker casket, which was described in the undertakers' glossy brochure as 'caringly and passionately hand-crafted'. It was covered in a carpet of antique dusty-pink roses called Amnesia and delicate cherry blossom with cascading ivy and looked like a fairy-tale garden. 'We want it to be pretty and almost magical – think Sleeping Beauty meets the Secret Garden – in Provence,' was my demandingly eccentric brief to the florist.

Adam had decided to have Giggle as part of our family procession today. It felt like an inspired decision, a way of making the event less daunting for the girls, softening the day's formality with a burst of uniqueness, just as Rach always did. It also felt symbolic of the life Rach had strived to create for herself – the full stop at the end of her journey.

The doorbell rang. Giggle rushed to greet the undertakers in their long black morning coats and tie-pins, assembled solemnly like prosperous members of the Victorian elite.

'I'm scared, Dad,' I whispered, as we filed silently out of the house. 'I don't know if I can do this.'

I glanced at the shiny cortège of cars. An elderly man was walking on the other side of the road, struggling against the cold in a thin anorak. He stopped when he saw the cars and made the sign of the cross before going on his way.

'Perhaps,' my dad said, resting a hand on my shoulder, 'today is not really for us. It's a performance, a public ritual. We will do our duty and then . . . return. To our own private grief.'

He had never mastered the art of writing a postcard. He hadn't the first clue how to tell someone a pet was not coming back. And he was prone to coming out with entirely the wrong thing around a deathbed. But when I heard those words I felt grateful to have my father here today.

The Lord's my Shepherd, I'll not want;
He makes me down to lie,
In pastures green; He leadeth me
The quiet waters by.

The church was teeming with Rach's friends, who hugged each other warmly. Many of them were professional couples in their thirties and forties with young families, and were trying to comprehend the idea of a life so similar to their own being extinguished overnight. There was none of the nostalgic laughter that comes with the inevitable conclusion of a long life. More a sense of incredulity.

Yea, though I walk in death's dark vale,
Yet will I fear no ill;

Until now hymns had always made me think of school assemblies, triggering memories of high-pitched vitality and covert sniggers. They'd taken on a darker hue today, with their references to God's kingdom and final sacrifices. I didn't look at the casket and its vast floral covering. I'd rather not acknowledge that it was Rach in there. A baby cried and her mother dashed out guiltily. *It's fine*, I wanted to say, *this is Rach's day, remember*. She hated it when people complained about babies crying. 'What do these assholes expect you to do, pop a Xanax in their bottle?'

And in God's house forevermore
My dwelling-place shall be.

There was the gentle shuffle of people reseating themselves. My heels echoed nosily on the stone slabs as I walked up to the brass eagle lectern, placing my speech on its outstretched wings.

'Hi, everyone. I had the privilege of knowing Rach all my life,' I began.

Afterwards, friends were kind about my tribute but some of them told me, 'Your voice sounded different. Like it wasn't you.' They were right. It wasn't me. I was playing the part of someone dealing stoically with grief, protected by a veil of artificial composure.

Mum had chosen a poem by Maya Angelou to be read out by her actor friend Hugh, who had driven us to intensive care that night. It was called 'When Great Trees Fall'.

I tried to imagine what Rach would have thought of the choices we'd made to sum up her life. I kept hearing her voice when we were initially going through options. 'Ugh, bit "quote you'd find in a crystals shop," Em,' I heard her say of one.

Hugh read out the Maya Angelou poem quietly and unadorned, not as a classically trained actor but simply as a friend. Just the way she would have liked.

Adam got up to deliver his tribute. I held Mimi's hand as she watched him say his final goodbyes. He talked about punching above his weight and their married life, which had started in this church twelve years before.

I thought about her decision to leave the ephemeral bubble of Shakespeare quotes, dusty theatre programmes, overdrafts and *bon viveurs*, and her new world of family holidays, dog walks and insurance policies. She'd made a kind of mermaid's choice in the end, leaving our native grotto for a life rooted on firmer land.

We'd picked a David Bowie song to close the service. Rach and I had a long-running joke about terrible songs to play at funerals. We referred to it as 'Now That's What I Call Funerals', our very own dark fantasy compilation. She would email me occasionally with new contenders. 'What's worse? "I Believe I Can Fly" or the *Titanic* one?'

The song we went for today was Bowie's 'Everyone Says "Hi"'. It was kind of bittersweet and moving without being sentimental. I liked the simple idea of all of the people here today just wanting to say hi. It even included a reference to being missed by 'your big fat dog'. It felt like the perfect way to say goodbye.

Chapter Nine

Christmas 2013

'So, this will be your second Christmas without Rachael. How are you feeling about it?' asked Sue.

'A bit shit,' I said. 'But I guess nothing will be as bad as the first one.'

I was sitting in my therapist's consulting room, though 'consulting room' makes it sound way too grand. There were no black leather Mies Van der Rohe couches or framed anatomical drawings of the brain. It was a sunny room in a suburban street with a comfy sofa and the sound of Ocado vans reversing outside.

My sister had been to see Sue many years before, and had always talked about her fondly. Rach and I had both dabbled in therapy over the years, although I'd never stuck to it – too expensive, waste of time, why rake over the past? I'd reached out to a grief counsellor a few months after Rach died but it felt slightly overwhelming. I sat there ploughing through endless 'previously in this season' plot summaries, trying to unpack our complex backstory, finding myself saying things like, 'No, that was my dad's *other* girlfriend. The

Russian one? The one linked with Colonel Gaddafi?' I just wanted to talk to someone who understood our family history and dynamics. I was tired of the fact that even our closest family friends and relatives didn't know the full truth. Everyone always got the performance. But Sue knew what went on without the scenery. I'd had a few sessions with her to help me through the initial shock but it was only eighteen months after Rach's death that I committed to seeing her every week.

Losing Rach had thrown up all sorts of difficult feelings, forcing me to confront some uncomfortable truths. Without my sister's stabilising presence, my shadowy status as visitor in other people's lives had been thrown into sharp relief. It felt as if my entire past and present had died along with her – but also my future. I didn't know who to be without Rach. 'Sometimes,' Sue said, 'it takes a traumatic incident to change who you are. Perhaps this is Rachael's lasting gift to you.'

She hadn't promised any overnight miracles. There were several luggage carousels' worth of baggage to unpack. But I found myself dropping the mask in a way I hadn't ever done to anyone else. Starting to challenge assumptions I'd always made about myself, cartoon characteristics that had been laid down in our family story. She forced me to unpick the childhood incidents I'd turned into anecdotes.

So. Christmas. Another one without Rach was never going to be a 'Let it snow!' celebration. More of a 'Gotta Get Through This' endurance test. But, as I said to Sue, it couldn't be as bad as last year.

The first Christmas after she died, I'd found myself having

a bit of a meltdown in Liberty's. The store was packed with men on lunch breaks frantically grabbing gift beauty sets. One middle-aged man was impatiently breaking off from his phone call to answer questions about wrapping. 'Yes, fine, all right, put one of your bow THINGS on it.' I reached instinctively for my phone to share 'one of your bow THINGS on it' with Rach. A new addition to our library of sayings.

And then I remembered. Habit had decided to have some fun overriding sanity – just for the hell of it. The seasonal music and smell of pine candles suddenly felt suffocating. I pushed through the double doors into the street and walked the tears off through Regent's Park until I got home.

This year we gathered on Christmas Day at Mum's. We'd powered through the slog of what bereaved people call 'Firsts'. First birthdays and anniversaries. First Mother's Day. We had established some post-Rach traditions, toasting 'Mummy Rachael', the name we encouraged two-year-old Bertie to use so that she has a sense that this person we talk about is her mum, even if she's not physically here. Adam wore a T-shirt saying 'Life Rolls On' and my mum cooked the roast potatoes the Gordon Ramsay way that Rach liked.

My mum also placed a life-sized cardboard cut-out of Justin Bieber in the living room: Mimi's very own Christ figure. As she was arranging tinsel around his neck, Mum's legs gave way and she grasped a chair for support. 'Pissed after one drink, darling!' she said. 'You'll have to put me to bed!'

She had lost weight recently. I was worried that she was skipping meals and remembered my own collapse at the hospital. 'You need to eat,' I urged her. 'You're too thin!'

She smiled, pointing out that that was an unlikely piece of advice from someone who worked for a fashion magazine.

My dad didn't come over for Christmas anymore. He was spending it with his girlfriend, who remained in his life. As revelations go, his sudden no-shows were hardly up there with Watergate but his absence stung slightly now. I was inclined to take it as a one-star review of our collective worth without Rach. And I suspected his absence was mainly my fault.

We'd had a series of difficult conversations since Rach died, about money, bailiffs and the general chaos of his life, which had gone into turbo-mode now that his faculties were dwindling. I was faced with angry creditors and legal notices as he attempted to get by on his old standbys of charm and false promises in a modern era when those qualities were no longer enough.

The chaos felt overwhelming without Rach to share the burden. Or to maintain order – we were like two angry street brawlers now that her moderating presence had left the ring. His girlfriend had kept an eye on his life admin in the initial aftermath of Rach's death but that period of grace was over. A few months afterwards, she had delivered a stack of brown envelopes to my house neatly labelled 'Dad's affairs'.

'Affairs? Well, at least he's finally owned up to them all,' my mother laughed.

I paid off his unpaid rent and my mum rallied into action, arranging for him to get state support.

'Splendid!' he said. 'I shall use the money for theatre tickets!'

'You'll end up in prison if you do that,' my mum pointed out.

'I will welcome the solitude. And I can end my days reading!'

He never had lost the art of a comeback.

Then he arranged to go to Greece with his girlfriend and called to ask me to pay for it. 'Just take the money out of the trust fund!' he said. The money left in trust to Rach and me by relatives had been plundered to virtually nothing over the years. Rach and I had signed documents to release funds well into adulthood. Business-class airfares, a series of loans.

'Look, I only need a few thou . . .' He paused briefly. 'It might well be my last holiday.'

I reluctantly agreed but took the opportunity to deliver some harsh home truths about his spending, urging him to prepare for his old age. He responded with fury. It reminded me of 'the one where Dad kicked the door down'. Eventually he hung up. He got his holiday but something shifted irrevocably after that heated conversation. We'd learned never to confront my father about difficult facts so it was a rash move to pull back the curtain and expose the man behind the Great Oz.

I initially felt that the onus was on me to patch it up. After all, I was the rational one who still had all their faculties. I knew that some of his friends who weren't privy to my clean-up operations and his habit of slipping in and out of our lives might cast me as a heartless villain. So I decided to give them what they wanted. I opted to treat his ghosting of me with defiance. I decided not to build any more bridges.

'I think I've worked out that my dad's just not that into me!' was my smart-mouthed, hot take on it, at least to the outside world.

Some of my friends suggested that he'd cut me off because

of the Alzheimer's. 'It can make people act out of character,' they gently offered.

I nodded politely rather than explaining that this was the way things had always been. I thought of him telling Rach and me all those years ago that he had never wanted children.

Funny how things turn out.

I arranged to take Mimi, who was now twelve, away to a country hotel for the weekend. She put on make-up for our posh dinner and fell excitedly upon the glitzy shower products. I almost didn't want to darken the atmosphere by raising the subject of loss. But I kept remembering what an ex-boyfriend once told me about losing his mother as a child, how he longed to know every detail, his need to make sense of it. I kept being told that it was important to share the difficult truths about Rach's death with Mimi rather than shroud everything in nostalgic vagueness. We discussed it over dinner and both had a little cry. It felt cleansing and I was relieved that I chose not to run away from it.

My mum had made memory boxes for the girls, on the advice of a children's bereavement charity. They were filled with letters from Rach's friends describing her, mementoes from her childhood and anecdotes written out on cards.

'Thank goodness no one ever made a memory box for me,' Mum said, and we both pondered what that might have contained. Deportation notices from the Egyptian embassy, prescriptions for amphetamines and legal advice about bigamy. Less a memory box, more a police evidence file, perhaps.

I tried to think of things that would lift Mimi's spirits. Jane arranged for her hairdresser to dye the tips of Mimi's hair pink, and I brought her huge piles of make-up samples from the beauty cupboard at work. 'L'Oreal Paris! That sounds posh,' she said, seizing upon a £2.99 hairspray and ignoring the Chanel eyeshadow palette.

She once told me that her only dream in life was to meet Justin Bieber. I wasn't sure I could make this happen – and even if I could, he seemed a bit unpredictable behaviour-wise. She was also a huge fan of Rihanna. So I raced into action when I found out that Rihanna was an upcoming guest on Jonathan's chat show. I talked to him and phoned his producer, Susie, and his celebrity booker, Sam. 'Look, I don't suppose there's ANY way . . .' I had never believed in angels – but I did after they quietly managed to sort it.

Mimi and I were trying hard not to stare open-mouthed at Rihanna's glossy and powerful legs escaping from a tiny tiered skirt as she shimmered her way towards us. Her hair was in blonde ringlets, poking out of a baseball cap. She brushed some strands out of her eye with lethal-looking black-tipped nails.

Her publicist whispered in her ear briefly as we stood in the studio corner watching her dazzling approach.

'Is this Mimi?' she said, crouching down to envelop Mimi in sweet fragrance. 'I've heard all about you, Mimi. And I hear you're an incredible little girl, you know that?'

I stood there as she engaged an awestruck Mimi in chat. And then I went and spoiled it all by doing something stupid like crying. I wiped away the tears but it was useless. Rihanna sees all.

'You're her aunt, right?' she said, rising up to stroke my cardiganed arm. 'It's okay, it's okay,' she said, looking momentarily confused about causing tears instead of the customary smiles.

'I honestly can't thank you enough,' I said in clipped tones, compensating for my temporary loss of British reserve.

She nodded and smiled at Mimi. 'Shall we go for a little walk?' she said, placing fingers glinting with gold jewellery inside Mimi's hand, as they wandered towards the green room, phone-wielding entourage scurrying behind.

You often see those pictures of people battling hardships meeting their heroes – pop stars leaning over hospital beds in expensive knitwear or footballers with starched kits posing alongside children. To be honest I'd always viewed them with incomprehension. Cynicism, even. Like meeting a famous person was going to change anything. How would encountering privilege make your pain better in any way?

But I thought about Mimi going to school tomorrow and I realised that in some small way, this had temporarily shifted her story. For a day, at least, she wouldn't be the girl whose mum died. She would be the girl who met Rihanna. So I got that whole hero meet-and-greet thing, now. Maybe it was a reminder that there was still joy to be had despite this bad thing that had happened. That tragedy didn't have to be the only thing that shaped you.

I had always been a bit meh about Rihanna. Not anymore. A few weeks after our encounter I heard someone half-heartedly weighing up some boots she was wearing, assessing her photo in a magazine. 'Not sure those boots really work,' they eventually offered. I think they're still recovering from my response.

I found it comforting going to Rach's house. It was exactly as she left it, the prints she lovingly framed, the wedding photos above the fireplace, the worn-down fabric on the sofa arm where she would place her laptop and Earl Grey tea. With Giggle at her feet, staring longingly at the forbidden land of the sofa.

'Giggle! Get down from there!' was still being shouted, just as it always was, and he responded as he always had, with the calculated doe-eyed look of the confidently irresistible.

I hadn't expected Giggle to be so important to the healing process. But back then I didn't know all the science behind dogs. That stroking them helped to lower stress hormones and release cuddly happy endorphins, oxytocin and serotonin. Getting these little doses of loveable energy from him felt like a shot of anti-depressant. He was just so consistently joyful and silly and familiar. Everything grief wasn't.

I couldn't help feeling that Giggle seemed to be experiencing his own form of loss. Friends had mentioned him whining at Rach's coffin during the funeral and even now, he sometimes curled up outside Rach's bedroom, head slumped on his paws like an exhausted train commuter table napping. Every time he raced to greet the doorbell or circled Rach's spot on the sofa I wondered what he made of her sudden disappearance.

'Do dogs mourn their owners?' was definitely something I had never predicted typing into Google one day. (But in fairness nor was 'I talk to my dead sister').

It turned out there was a fundamental difference between the way dogs and adult humans grieved. Dogs are emotionally and mentally wired to live in the eternal present with no sense of the future. So they experienced loss as a sustained forlorn waiting rather than a permanent absence. Basically, they never quite give up on the idea that the person might return. So as far as Giggle was concerned, Rach lived eternally in the now. Her current absence had not drawn a line under her entire existence. To him, she would always be a part of our lives. And I liked that idea.

Giggle also reinforced routine, a foothold you cling to when you're buffeted around by trauma. He was the embodiment of Adam's 'Life Rolls On' T-shirt. It was a delicate high-wire act, mourning someone. Respecting grief without falling into an abyss. People say there's no way round it, you have to walk through it. So I tried to accept the unheralded moments of raw distress, which often arrive when you least want them to. During a brunch with the radio-show team, when the menu started to swim. Or at a screening of *ET* where the tug of nostalgia erupted into anguish. Even the simple question, 'Do you have any brothers or sisters?' sent me into panic, as I weighed up whether or not to burden a stranger with my tale. But grief had the power to block out the light so completely that you became accustomed to its dark familiarity. Which meant you had no option but to cling to the routine of daily life.

Giggle's predictability felt incredibly reassuring. You knew he'd react with greedy anticipation before every meal. He never turned down a walk. He would always try to jump onto the furniture, no matter how many times he got knocked back. His was a solid, unwavering presence. The symbol of a life with roots – the tiny heartbeat at the core of the dog families.

I loved it when he licked my nose with his pink tongue, his two wonky teeth poking out from his Gruffalo underbite. Sometimes he would leap out of my lap if he heard a noise in the garden, shifting into the code-red mode of a secret service agent. There was no transition from our peaceful sofa moment to sniffing around the flowerbeds, ears pricked, head twisting to check out swooping birds. *Oh, you're still in SOFA world*, his eyes said, with the condescension of a child finally abandoning its parents at the school gates. *What about all this exciting shit happening out here?*

'People always talk about living in the moment. But they rarely do,' the intensive-care consultant had told me. But watching Giggle racing from one fresh experience to another, I realised that dogs really did possess this gift. A stern word was instantly forgotten with the promise of a walk; the sofa would always be his Camelot, no matter how many times he was told his name wasn't on the list. This was why dog trainers explained that it was pointless to reprimand a dog for a mess on the carpet. They were fundamentally unable to link that thing they did five minutes ago with you being cross now. Dogs could not exist in anything but the moment.

Sometimes, sitting with the girls, I was hit with a sense of the injustice that Rach wasn't watching Bertie take her first steps. Or enjoying Mimi discovering *Fawlty Towers* on YouTube. I worried about having meltdowns in front of them but tried to remember some good advice I got from Alun, my radio-show colleague, who lost his dad as a child. 'Their mum died,' he said. 'It IS sad. Hiding grief tells them it's wrong to be sad.'

So I tried to be honest with them if I was having a moment. Tell them I was just thinking about Rach and how much we all missed her. Mimi always reached out to hug me, as Giggle clambered up to join us, licking away the tears with an impressive thoroughness. I'd never quite worked out what prompted dogs to do that. Was it genuine empathy or just because they liked the salt? My head told me it might have been the salt in Giggle's case – he really was a greedy bastard. But my heart couldn't help but hope that maybe he was just looking out for all of us.

I wanted to get a puppy. My mum was an enthusiastic enabler, although she frowned slightly at some of my choices as we looked through galleries of Pomeranians and Malteses and poodles on her computer. 'Oh, darling, do be careful with little dogs,' she said. 'Some of them look like they belong to those nasty old women who still say "the coloureds."'

I researched the chow chow, those gloriously regal, cinnamon-furred Chinese dogs, with blue tongues and sloping eyes that made them look permanently grumpy from interrupted sleep. There was a litter due shortly, I discovered. I wanted to call mine Septimus. 'Sounds like a nasty infection,' laughed a colleague.

'These things?' said Frank's partner, Cathy, when I showed her a picture. 'They're fucking MASSIVE!'

Jane's dad, Stu, was very wary. 'I knew a chow chow once. It was a real asshole.'

Choosing a dog was a bit like sharing prospective baby names – everyone had their own history with a spiteful Naomi or a Liam who stole their lunch money.

But it wasn't everyone else that stopped me from taking the final step and welcoming Septimus the 'real asshole' into my life. It was me. I did what I had always done with decisions involving definitive life choices – stall. I preferred not to address the real reasons behind those breezy deadline extensions. Even though I knew exactly what they were.

When you defined yourself entirely by how you relate to others – the daughter of two impressively noisy characters, the sister of an even-tempered guardian, the friend of driven outliers – it was impossible to know what your own world looked like. So you stood aside, witnessing everyone else building a life filled with things that shaped them.

Maybe it was enough to get brief hits of dog ownership through Giggle. I would leave it a bit, until the time was right.

But there was a funny thing about the right time – it never came.

Chapter Ten

February 2014

'Darling, are you on your way to work?'

'I'm so late, Mum! Can I call you back?'

'Don't worry. I'll tell you later.'

'Is it about your Whistles jumper? I'll drop it off—'

'Darling, it's not good. I've got sodding motor neurone disease.'

A bus juddered to a halt right by me, its noisy engine drowning out the teenagers swearing and shoving each other. The doors concertinaed back with a hiss as the driver glanced at my frozen form. With an irritated sigh he manoeuvred his huge red chariot back to his journey.

Sodding motor neurone disease. Of course that was how she would break the news. A baked potato left too long in the oven got the status of 'fucking buggery bollocks, this is a disaster of the highest order!' But a fatal degenerative disease was only a 'sodding'.

I knew she wanted to give the diagnosis the contempt it

deserved, denying it the honour of anything more than a mild swear word. The defiant optimist again. I had challenged her over this approach to Rach's diagnosis. But that was not my right, now. We were no longer helpless witnesses to horror, navigating it together. Now it was her story, so she got to decide the tone.

I sensed that she didn't want me to collapse. So the only vulnerability I revealed was by lapsing into the use of the word 'Mummy', something I hadn't done since childhood. I was drawn suddenly to its cosy intimacy. 'Muuum!' was what we shouted down the stairs when we had no clean pants. Or what we said with a sigh when she used phrases like 'Brillo pads!' several decades after their use ceased to be acceptable. 'Muum!' was hurled impatiently during a Trivial Pursuit game when she insisted with tipsy defiance that Neil Armstrong's first words on the moon were 'Merry Christmas, everyone!'

It didn't feel right to use the dismissively adolescent 'Mum' today.

She had told me not to go with her to the hospital appointment this morning. We had been to so many over the past two months. 'It'll just be more of the same endless tedium!' she assured me. I felt terrible that she had had to absorb the first impact of this news alone. I thought of her making her way down the hospital steps with this sentence suddenly laid on her shoulders.

'We're getting like the bloody Kennedys, darling, aren't we?' she said. 'It's ridiculous.'

I tried to mimic her spirited stoicism, reaching for the sort of comforting phrases that people use to accompany bad news even if they never quite believe them. 'At least we know what it is now,' I said.

But we both knew that actually, the 'not knowing' was a period we would look back to with misty water-coloured nostalgia, compared to what was ahead. During our various conversations with neurologists, MND had been mentioned as something they were keen to rule out. I knew it was not an easy way to go. It meant the gradual loss of speech, movement, swallowing and finally breathing. It also moved fairly quickly. Stephen Hawking's story was greeted with weariness by consultants as they patiently pointed out that he was a medical outlier who defied the odds.

It felt almost laughable that fate would have the sheer balls to strike when we were still reeling from the last disaster. I had always sort of assumed your future was overseen by a rational show runner. One who would dismiss the plausibility of another central character being written out so soon after the previous end-of-season shocker. It seemed our one had lost it, and decided to wrong-foot the audience entirely. 'Hang on, what if . . . we threw those characters another sucker punch? When they're still on the ropes? *That'd* be a finale.'

Though perhaps I should have seen this latest twist coming. 'Do you know, darling, sometimes I feel I've sort of given up a bit since we lost Rach,' Mum told me a few months after the funeral, as we climbed the hill up to Sainsbury's. 'I know that must be hard for you. I'm sorry.'

I had felt the rush of triggered childhood shame. Of course she had given up. She had been left with the crappy black swan. But I forced myself to sit with the discomfort and just said, 'I know. I kind of have, too.' We had both on the surface been managing to trudge through each day, but with a vaguely wounded resignation, like the last couple at the dance marathon, half-heartedly dancing on, not wanting to let the other one down.

I'd had a sense for a while that something wasn't quite right with Mum. She had started to drag her feet oddly, lose her balance, slur her words a bit. At first I just thought she was hitting the Prosecco a bit too hard, self-medicating. And not eating enough. I had no idea that losing her footing as she put tinsel on Justin Bieber was a sign of something sinister.

But then things rapidly got more pronounced and we decided to investigate, re-entering the world of hospital waiting rooms and lanyard-wearing consultants.

'It's detective work really, you have to eliminate the suspects!' a consultant neurologist said, smiling and furiously making notes with his fountain pen.

'You're like Sherlock Holmes! No morphine addiction, I hope,' my mum replied, with playful theatricality, not anticipating his reaction – which was an uncomfortable silence.

'Miserable old bastard,' she muttered on the way out. 'Sense of humour *nul points*.'

'*Nul points*' was another one of her slightly obsolete 'Brillo pads' phrases that Rach and I teased her about, a cultural throwback to Eighties Eurovision Song Contests.

As her symptoms progressed over the next few months, we didn't address the emotional implications of her diagnosis. 'I am not going to stick to the script that has been written for me. I refuse to be gloomy!' she said, throwing herself into practicalities, making her will, selling her house, asking me to look into a care flat for her where she could have twenty-four-hour help. 'I'll ham up the limping when we visit so I can jump the waiting list!'

She told me that she wanted to stay close to Rach, and by some miracle the following month I found an independent care flat close to Highgate Cemetery. She bought fresh white linen for her special hoist bed, which she called 'very Playboy Mansion!' and filled the stark medical bathroom with antique fragrance bottles. She decorated the living room with a collage of Rach and a mountain of toys for Bertie's visits. By the time she moved in, she was dependent on her wheelchair, which she threatened to decorate with gold baubles at Christmas.

We were sitting in her flat some months later, having tea with one of Rach's old friends and looking through old photos, when we got a call to say that Aunty Lyn had died from a brain haemorrhage.

'I feel guilty, Em,' Mum said sadly. 'She kept calling. But I didn't want her to see me like this.'

Lynsey had stayed in touch after the Holly Village days, turning up at birthdays in a cloud of scent, sharing tales of her latest romantic exploits and reaching out with kindness when Rach died. But Mum's chosen role of adoring courtier perhaps required levels of energy she simply didn't have anymore.

We went to her funeral with Jane and her mum, Mandy. It was attended by various faces from archive editions of *Top of the Pops*, some white-haired with walking sticks, some defying old age with leather trousers and hair dye. After the service we wandered over with fellow guests to pay our respects at the grave, where her casket lay. It was at that point I realised that I was still something of a rookie when it came to navigating wheelchairs. The wheels got stuck in mud by the six-foot open drop, threatening to throw Mum straight on to the lily-covered casket below.

'I can't move it out!' I hissed to Jane.

'Oh fuck! Let me try,' Jane hissed back.

Jane valiantly wrestled the wheelchair away from the kind of scene that wins 'funniest sitcom moments EVER!' compilations, while mourners looked over with slight confusion. With a final jerk, Jane managed to free Mum from the dark comic denouement that beckoned.

'Well, that would have been quite the tribute,' my mum said as we all giggled about our narrow brush with dark disaster during the car ride back to her flat.

'I loved laughing with Jane and Mandy about the wheelchair,' she said, when we got back home. 'I wish everyone would be more like that with me. I need laughter, not gloomy sympathy.'

We reminisced about Lynsey's best bits. I recalled a phrase she used a lot. 'Life's too short and so am I.' I told Mum that it was a good epitaph. If Lynsey hadn't nabbed it already, I was stealing it for mine.

My mum smiled. 'You bastard. I wanted that.'

'I can't believe your mum's going through this so soon after you've lost Rach,' friends told me. I felt almost embarrassed that they had to bear this fresh burden. I worried that I was burning through my credit with them. I'd turned into a talisman for bad luck. The raven darkening a family picnic. The skull in the Renaissance painting reminding you of mortality. But in some ways bad news had become the new normal, the forest fire that continued to rage after the rain, intent on destroying everything in its wake. I treated it with acceptance throughout the day, absorbing the admiration people threw my way ('You're so brave!'), relieved to be seen as capable and in control. It was only at night that I was hit with the sense of being the last woman standing, the one who forgot to call a cab in time, loitering alone in the street as the others headed off. When I was having one of my 'kitchen floor' parties – they were back – as usual, I allowed the calls to go straight to voicemail. I wanted to make my anguish palatable, to have a 'good' grief, be a healthy mourner, someone impressively stoical in the face of upheavals.

I hadn't expected the next phase of loss – the 'manic bursts of carpe diem' stage, when I was driven to impulsive surges of abandon. But I could kind of work out what was going on – I was getting busy living instead of dying. Sue seemed to think it was totally to be expected, which reassured me. And besides, it was much more fun.

I started saying yes to everything. A twenty-four-hour trip to Barcelona for a fashion party in honour of Kate Moss? I'd be there! A taxi straight from Heathrow to the opening of a pop-up restaurant in a disused petrol station? Why not?

'Disused petrol station – it's almost as good as that invite to "drinks in an abandoned Bulgarian swimming baths,"' I said to the handsome young TV and movie idol sat next to me.

We spent the rest of the evening laughing over our Peruvian ceviche and paprika octopus, swapping stories about the absurdities of the fashion industry and eccentric actors. He was the sort of man whose face regularly graced magazine covers and who got romantically linked with hot young things, so his presence at the event invoked an unspoken social contract of sharing. No one was allowed to hog the golden karaoke mike all night.

I made gestures to liberate him as dinner ended, but he grabbed a bottle of wine and said, 'I fancy a smoke, shall we move this outside?'

I was aware of suspicious glances from other guests as I greedily overstayed my allotted time with the golden karaoke mike. Perhaps they were wondering why he had decided to grant a forty-something woman an impromptu one-on-one. I wasn't entirely sure myself. But I realised that I didn't care. This new phase, the 'fuck it, the worst already happened' one, had gifted me a strange defiance. I felt like a superhero who was slowly adjusting to their secret power – boldness.

I was enjoying chatting away to this stranger, who didn't know my 'poor Em' backstory. It was also tearing down some of the received wisdom about ageing that I'd never questioned, which women of my generation were fed as truths. That you become invisible and stripped of power without your youthful beauty. That in a room like this, filled with glowing twenty-five-year-olds, you had no currency. The actor didn't interrogate me about why I didn't have children. He didn't even ask how old I was. He didn't seem to have a cougar kink. His untarnished acceptance of me, purely as he found me, was almost weird. Turns out disused petrol stations could be handy for epiphanies.

He seized my phone to exchange numbers and over the next few weeks we swapped friendly texts as he extended hopelessly impractical invitations, which pinged up at odd hours. 'Come to NYC!' 'Just landed in LA – when am I seeing you for a messy night out?' 'Come to Soho house – NOW!'

I didn't take him up on any of the offers to join his crew of pals on their bar crawls. Mainly because I didn't have assistants on call to facilitate travel arrangements at an hour's notice. But his perception of me – as an entertaining new gang member who could dash to New York on the strength of a text – had shifted something. It allowed me to see myself as a colourful peacock rather than the raven. As someone who might inspire a drunken welcome instead of worried glances. And not as a woman running out of time – just a person, lucky to still have time.

I threw my new fuck-it persona back into socialising and dating. I didn't wait shyly for invites or agonise over potential rejection. I had the newly acquired confidence of an Olympic athlete, parading his medal on a post-victory boys' night out.

I met a man in his twenties. I had to fight the old me rising up to whisper, *what will people say about the age gap?* For once I tried to trust my feelings rather than my fears. He was kind and caring and, best of all, utterly hilarious.

'Isn't it odd when he doesn't get any of your references?' someone asked. Indicating that a thorough knowledge of *Minder* episodes was the best basis for a fulfilling relationship. It was a view that was not only irrelevant – turned out he was obsessed by *Minder* – it was also inaccurate. I discovered that interesting people tend not to dismiss things purely on the grounds that they haven't personally lived through them.

I'd forgotten what it was like to laugh like this, the uncontrolled kind that gets less frequent in middle age. The sort of helpless laughter that Rach and I enjoyed together. He filled a hotel suite with thoughtful gifts and flowers for my birthday, a brief escape from my world of hospice corridors and complicated medical procedures. He bought me a toy Bagpuss after I told him about Rach's habit of quoting the show's catchphrase, 'But Emily still loved him', to tease me over a crush. It made me smile and then unleashed something more raw, a small kitchen-floor party, which I hadn't exposed to anyone before. He comforted me until it passed but I worried about how overwhelming all this must be for him. My problems of death and loss and illness had been thrust onto the first third of his life's story, hurtling him into the final chapters.

Things eventually came to an end after a few honest, soul-searching discussions. We simply realised that we were at different points on our respective journeys. We said our goodbyes and agreed to give each other space for the next few months, so that we could heal. 'I'm still wearing the trainers he bought me. That's a good sign that I don't harbour any bad feeling,' I told a fashion colleague. 'Yeah,' she said. 'It helps that they're Gucci.'

I didn't stay single for long. Manic-carpe-diem people don't. A man invited me out to dinner. He was erudite and charming. A glass of champagne was waiting for me when I arrived at the smart Knightsbridge restaurant. We enjoyed that early-days bubble of courtship, climbing those first rungs on the ladder of a joint narrative, living the things that become part of your tapestry. That time when we handed over our Valentine's gifts and discovered we had bought each other the same book. The anecdote he shared with friends about coming to me for fashion advice and getting the damning response, 'Short-sleeved shirt? Bit "coach driver".'

Things moved fast. Two months into our relationship he suggested we go on holiday to the Maldives. My mum's health was deteriorating and I discussed with her and her doctors whether I could realistically consider a week-long break.

She now relied mainly on an electronic tablet to write down her thoughts. 'PLEASE GO DARLING!' she wrote frantically. 'OR I WILL BE UPSET. Room for my wheelchair in the villa?'

He brought a warm, dependable decisiveness to my life, visiting the hospice with me, leaving energy bars in my bag to make sure I ate. I felt protected when he supported me over an upsetting email I got not long after we returned from holiday.

A friend of my mother's felt that I had made the wrong decisions over Mum's medical care, and questioned my attitude. She mentioned a message I had sent my mum where I'd said, 'Hope you're feeling okay.' She quoted this. 'Okay? On no account imagine she is "okay".' She told me I wasn't giving my mother enough 'TLC'. 'Over to you, darling!' she signed off.

I imagined the conversations everyone must be having. 'Rachael would have been kinder. Made better decisions. Emily left her mother in a hospice to go to the Maldives. Can you believe it? What a selfish bitch.'

I went to see Sue.

'I visit Mum all the time,' I said. 'I talk to her carers, I have meetings with the hospice doctors, I take her to the toilet. Why isn't it enough?'

'Why do you automatically assume guilt, Emily?' asked Sue.

'Because I've always felt I'm bad. It doesn't matter how much I try to change.'

'You have changed. Since you lost Rachael you are starting to shape your own identity outside of your family history. People can find change unsettling.'

'It's just so hard not having Rach here. She always got it.'

'Maybe it's because Rachael's not here that this is happening. You need three people to continue triangulating – not two. Perhaps your mother's friend is now fulfilling that third role between the two of you.'

I thought about what she had said, about the way things always were – the female triangle we formed, which Sue told me often resulted in people acting out roles. Victim, persecutor and rescuer. I realised that I had become used to the role of persecutor. And after a while it was easier to accept it rather than push against it. My blooper reel got rolled out to people alongside Rach's highlights and I lived up to being the person presented in the edit. That was the only character my mother's friend knew, the person she sent that email to.

For the first time ever I chose to resist the triangle. I didn't reply to the email. My friend Polly called it the equivalent of a WhatsApp notification announcing 'this person has left the group'. The email wasn't mentioned again and the drama subsided of its own accord – you had to fan the blaze for it to spread. I was sitting in the cab on the way to the hospice a few days later when the song 'When You Say Nothing At All' came on Magic FM. I decided that Ronan Keating was actually the true father of modern-day psychology.

27 February 2015

My mum was on large doses of pain relief with a ventilator to help her breathe. I was sitting by her bedside in the hospice lifting moist sponges to her lips, just as I had for Rach.

I flicked through her notebook while she slept, the one she sometimes used to write things down for me and the doctors. 'More drugs!!' was scrawled in black felt-tip across several pages. 'Can they help hurry things UP???? There are ways, darling . . .'

It wasn't the only time she had talked to me about wanting to die. 'Can they not bump me off!' she had managed to half croak, half laugh last week.

'That's a huge step just to get a mini-break in Switzerland, Mum,' I replied. She smiled.

I agreed to sign a 'do not resuscitate' declaration for her. I also told her that I understood if she had made her peace with going, and that I would be okay. 'Thank you, my darling,' she said. 'I think I'm ready.'

It was getting late. John, Mum's boyfriend, arrived and sat quietly in the corner of the room. He arrived at exactly the same time every day. If he was early he sat outside, checking his watch. My boyfriend had been touched by it yesterday, when we spotted him. 'Some people need routine to make sense of the world,' he said. 'If he says 5.00pm it has to be 5.00pm.' I understood why he needed to do that. Especially now.

I watched my mother breathing.

She opened her eyes and pointed to her bag on the plastic hospice chair.

I delved into it. 'Diary?'

She shook her head. She tapped her collarbone repeatedly.

'Necklace?' She made a cheery thumbs up, the kind of cheesy photocall gesture that didn't sit comfortably with an end of days request. Which was why it couldn't be more her. I pulled out her gold St Christopher's from the inside pocket. 'Let me put it on you,' I said, loosening the clasp.

She pushed the necklace back into my hand.

I stroked the tiny gold pendant with its raised relief of the saint with a staff, that she had worn for as long as I could remember. It was for protection throughout life's journey.

'Thank you, Mum,' I said, fastening it around my neck. 'I've always had my eye on this!'

She smiled and took my hand, before disappearing into sleep.

28 February 2015

The nurse greeted me the next morning with the gentle tone I'd come to recognise. 'I think your mum's on her way.'

But I was already an expert on what someone's final moments looked like – the altered tone of her skin, the drained colour, the odd sense of absence were all familiar. My boyfriend held my hand by her bed as we watched her slip away.

I realised that over the previous few months I had entered

a peaceful place with my mum. The sharp edges between us had softened; the baggage of the past felt lightened. It had been helped by me throwing myself into a life with someone who wasn't connected to my family identity. But also, perhaps, when you knew someone wasn't going to be around for much longer that forced you to focus on your relationship now. Not the past.

My boyfriend discreetly left me to say my private goodbyes. I told Mum that I loved her.

I knew what the deal was now. The death certificates, the caskets, the hymns, the phone calls, the unexpected pockets of sadness. Sorting through her bag and finding her glasses wrapped in a piece of suede fabric. An old folded piece of paper fell out of her lilac diary. 'Dear mummy,' it read, 'thank you for the pram. Katy wanted a pram so it is good. You are very generos!!! Love Rach XXXXX'.

12 March 2015

Bryce, the priest we had for Rach's funeral, conducted the service. He opened with the bold choice of 'I did tell Emily that we must stop meeting like this,' which landed slightly awkwardly among the mourners. They seemed unsure whether it was appropriate to snigger at the double loss today represented. But to me it felt like a suitably irreverent way to send her off and I filed it away with the other anecdotes in our family archive, of which I was now sole custodian.

My dad was at the service with his girlfriend, who now preferred to be called simply his 'friend'. I wondered whether today would allow a thaw in relations between us. But I didn't find out. They left straight after the service and didn't come to the wake.

'His girlfriend said she was taking him home because he was very upset,' explained a family friend.

'We're all upset. That's kind of the deal at a funeral,' I said archly.

I chose not to access the hurt I felt inside that he didn't stay to talk to me.

I hadn't been especially welcoming, introducing him briefly to my boyfriend with a strained hello. Even my mum's relationship with him had tailed off when her health declined and she lacked the energies to focus on his life admin. His presence in our lives had been entirely maintained by her, I realised. So now he had simply disconnected from our world.

He didn't feature much in my eulogy today, an omission I justified by deciding that it would be unfair to her old boyfriend John, who had remained in her life, waiting dutifully in the wings for his calls.

'Quotes from Socrates aren't that useful when you need help with a blocked toilet,' Rach used to say, comparing our father's role in her life to John's. I paid tribute in my speech to John's loyalty and enduring love. It was only some time afterwards that I considered this was a pointed slight to my father. My very own Mark Antony moment, fulsomely praising one individual in order to condemn another. The hurt bubbling underneath managing to find the surface, however much you bury it.

Chapter Eleven

I focused on building a life with my boyfriend, meeting his family, involving him in my friendship group, enjoying how much he made Mimi and Bertie laugh. We talked about the dog we might get one day. Our relationship was like a slice of tavern-based light relief in a corpse-strewn Shakespearean tragedy.

But I was struggling to process the losses. I fell over at work one day with dizzy spells, and a colleague took me to A&E. Hospitals in the London area were becoming my *Mastermind* specialist subject. The doctors explained that it was actually a cocktail of low blood pressure, anxiety and stress. I was slightly embarrassed that it was simply my mental state that had caused this dramatic overnight stay in hospital.

'This isn't what he signed up for, is it,' I laughed to one of my boyfriend's female friends when we had dinner with her a week later. 'We should still be at the cocktails and romance stage!'

I arranged a birthday dinner with my friends to acknowledge all the support they'd shown me. My boyfriend stood up to list the reasons he loved me, and I felt as if I was leaving bear country and finally entering dog world, at long last.

'I'm so happy to see you in sunshine after all that cloud,' Frank texted me the following day.

'It was the birthday I always dreamed of having but never thought I would!' I replied.

A few weeks later, in a denouement I hadn't seen coming, my boyfriend suddenly ended our relationship. He wrote in his email that it was nothing I had done. His life just didn't accommodate a partner right now. He offered to meet up to say our final goodbyes in person but my friends adamantly advised against a post-mortem, suggesting it was like an alcoholic popping into the off-licence for one last browse.

Over the following few weeks and months my ex sent texts. He hoped we could still stay civil and remain friends. But I decided to stay clean and resist that one harmless beer, aware of the hangover on the other side.

'I feel guilty sometimes, like a bad person for cutting off contact,' I told Sue.

'But you're healing, and acting authentically. Contacting someone just to seem likeable – that would be dishonest.'

'It will make people think that I'm unreasonable, the bad ex.'

'But you know the truth. So do all the people that care about you. Is it important what outsiders think?'

'Sometimes I think that's all I am. Other people's opinions of me.'

'And the people you are drawn to as friends, the Franks, let's say. Do they care what people think of them? Do they want to be liked and seen as nice?'

'No. I'm almost in awe of that kind of honesty. But Frank told me once it's a harder way to live.'

'It is. But once you start you can't really ever go back. Boundaries and self-care don't make you a bad person.'

Once the pain of romantic disappointment began to recede, my old pal 'complicated grief' returned to my life, and this time it was a houseguest who had come armed with a list of squatters' rights. Grief can be really annoying like that, a bad date who just won't get the hint.

Frank put this blast of fresh pain down to having had 'a pain-killer, something good to think about when everything else seemed bleak. And then it suddenly got withdrawn. Leaving you with all the original bereavement plus cold turkey. That's double tough.' He signed off his email, 'Right. That'll be nine guineas, please.'

He was right, as he so often was (with the exception of that time he decided to get a gold tooth). Perhaps I had simply traded being a sister and a daughter for being a girlfriend. And now I was worried about feeling like nobody again.

Sue helped me to make sense of it all but I felt I needed some other kind of help as well. I went to my doctor and told her I thought I needed anti-depressants for a bit. 'I am having therapy but this feeling . . . It's out of control. Like the past couple of years have taken their toll.'

She turned away suddenly from the constant keyboard-tapping that characterises modern GP visits and looked at me with concern. 'You've had multiple losses. Of course you feel out of control.'

She agreed to prescribe me some low-dose anti-depressants. 'Kind of like faking it till I make it, I guess,' I suggested.

'Absolutely,' she said. 'And then we'll review it. I think you're going to be okay, you know. Asking for help is a good sign.'

A few weeks later I went to Highgate Cemetery to finalise arrangements for my mum's grave plot, just a couple of tree-lined paths away from Rach's limestone monument. My ex-boyfriend had helped me pick out the spot. It was in a little shaded area filled mainly with children's memorials and the grave of the actor, Bob Hoskins. That seemed right for her.

Highgate Cemetery felt a bit like an afterlife private members' club. It was filled with artsy names and you needed a membership card to gain entry. I was on first-name terms with the gravedigger by then (whose job title must be due for a modern upgrade to 'post-life consultant') and he pointed out well-loved regulars. 'Lucian Freud over there. George Michael's mother. We get them all!'

The cemetery administrator greeted me cheerily and handed me the grave paperwork to look over. I realised that my ex-boyfriend's name was still alongside mine as joint life-custodian of the plot. 'Actually . . . it's just me now,' I said.

He paused briefly, pen poised in mid-air, without looking up, before amending it diplomatically. 'There we go! All ready,' he said brightly. 'Super spot you've chosen for Mum.'

My friends swaddled me in protective concern. They got me through the days, as did the welcome dose of my new pal Sertraline and the distraction of office life. But a grimy Instagram filter had settled on my worldview, washing out all vividness. It just wouldn't shift.

I was over at the girls' a few days later, for Mimi's birthday. Bertie was playing with her *Frozen* jigsaw, Mimi was checking her Snapchat messages. Giggle came over to join us, reaching up to lick my face before squatting at my feet. I scooped him into my arms and stroked his belly. Adam was making me tea in that oversize sports mug that always sat oddly in their Farrow and Ball haven. He padded around the kitchen with 6 Music blaring. I tried to remember the words the consultant in the intensive care unit had said to me. *People rarely live in the moment.*

'Today is a happy day because it's your birthday and I'm here with you,' I said with slightly forced gaiety to Mimi.

'Will you go home and cry after you leave, E?' said Bertie suddenly.

And Mimi and I laughed in the way you do, when a four-year-old totally had you nailed.

October 2015

I was at my desk, editing a piece on 'This season's MUST-have accessories!' surrounded by the gentle hum of office life.

My mobile rang. I didn't recognise the number.

'Emily? It's Gregory.'

Gregory was one of my dad's closest friends, the only person who remained a permanent fixture in his life. While most people had struggled to keep up with his peripatetic chaos, Gregory had found a way to view him with tolerant affection. His forgiving stance threw my exasperated absence into sharp relief and I assumed he'd been given an unflattering portrait of me. I steeled myself for a difficult discussion.

'Emily, it's your dad. He collapsed in a café. He's in hospital. I think he's dying. I'm so sorry.'

My workmates responded with concern but disbelief. *What, again?* their glances conveyed. I'd made no secret of the fact that my father and I were estranged, so they clearly weren't sure whether the standard sympathy that accompanied news of a dying parent was appropriate.

I grabbed my jacket and, out of sheer habit, sprayed myself with the perfume on my desk. The scent hit me in sickly, vulgar waves on my way down in the lift, as if I'd defiantly refused to honour this news with the respect it deserved. A sweet colleague had offered to order me a cab but I told her I wanted to clear my head with a walk. 'I need to make some calls,' I said. That last bit was a lie. I had no one I needed to tell. It was just me with my new persistent stalker, complicated shock.

Autumn had arrived and office workers darted across Blackfriars Bridge, confronting the breeze by clutching their suit jackets tighter. They laughed into phones and dodged cycles with impatient purpose. They would get that call about a father one day, if they hadn't already. I imagined them phoning loved ones as they rushed to unite in collective grief around the family patriarch. Hugging, getting each other coffees and taking turns to keep vigil, bonded over their loss. Consoling each other with memories before returning to their own lives, altered by grief but not consumed with a lonely dark shame. That was not how the dog families, the normal people, lived.

When I got to the hospital lobby there was a film crew rushing around with an air of vague entitlement. A woman in a suit fiddled with an earpiece and read through some notes. She smiled sympathetically when she saw my grave face and swift pace. *Sorry for intruding on your pain with this trivia*, her look said. I felt fraudulent. I didn't deserve the respectful glance she had thrown me.

I had called some of my friends. Jane was supportive and offered to come back from her work trip in Leeds but I insisted that she didn't need to. Daisy my producer was sympathetic and Polly was at home nearby. 'I can be there in twenty minutes.' She arrived dispensing hugs and love and I was relieved to have an ally here, to protect me from the potential crew of angry villagers with flaming torches. But Gregory was calm and compassionate when he showed me into a cubicle in the critical-care unit.

My dad's eyes were closed tightly as he breathed the deep sighs of the heavily medicated.

'He had a stroke. They've dosed him up on morphine but they've said they're not sure how long it will be now. I'm sorry,' Gregory said softly, putting an arm around me.

I knew from my recent crash course in the end stages of life that Dad had entered a place from which he was unlikely to return. He looked crumpled and unshaven; his white whiskery chin suggested a lack of daily self-care that was heartbreaking. I imagined him in his local café when his life juddered to its conclusion. Probably with his copy of *The Times*, a cup of tea and a cake, quoting Shakespeare to bemused waitresses, still grasping fragments of his life as a celebrated intellectual, dazzling people with eloquence in a TV studio.

When we were children he used to read us Shelley's poem 'Ozymandias'. We were drawn to its silly-sounding name rather than its treatment of the ephemeral nature of greatness. He encouraged us to quote from it, 'Look on *my works*, ye mighty, and *despair*!' every time we drove past a ruin or a derelict house. The childhood game popped into my mind now as I thought of his once formidable mind, robbed of its faculties, falling into nothingness. But I reminded myself that I had surrendered my right to feel sentimental over his last hours. It was as preposterous as the woman who put the cat in the bin respectfully placing flowers at the scene.

I spent the next twenty-fours reacquainting myself with the critical-care vigil routine, the hushed tones of nurses, the bowl with a sponge, the long nights. A handful of visitors arrived to say their goodbyes. Joan Bakewell, who was loyal to the last, and finally, Anita, who sounded the death knell of my parents' marriage. Her expensive clothes and refined presence emphasised the chasm between his old world and the depleted existence he finally led. She seemed kind and sensitive. I found out that she had bought him a TV not long ago and had kept a concerned eye on him over the years.

Perhaps it had been easier for us all to lay the blame at her feet rather than address the deeper truth: that my father simply never wanted a part in a domestic tableau. The home-wrecking monster of my childhood turned out to be a decent woman who had come here today quietly to pay her final respects.

Evening arrived. I lifted the sponge to his mouth regularly, wiped his face and stroked his brow, just the way I had with Rach and Mum. I thought of something a university boyfriend once said to me that had always stayed in my mind. 'I can play football. Rich can fix a car, among other things,' he had said, gesturing to our fellow student, who was expertly rolling a joint.

'But what can you actually DO, Em?' I answered him now, twenty-five years later. I had found my skill. I was a world-class expert in the last moments of life.

'Hey, Dad, your mouth's all dry,' I said, wiping the sponge across his lips.

And then his eyes opened. He looked at me for just a few seconds. He seemed confused, slightly stunned. But there was something else. Relief. *You came*, his fleeting gaze seemed to say.

We would never get to have our final chat, to put our differences aside and mend the flaming bridges that divided us. And I couldn't pretend that this moment had successfully buried the past. But it felt significant – perhaps more than any long-drawn-out conversation ever could have been.

It was 3.00am. The dark silence was broken by the sound of equipment humming in the ward. I huddled up on a chair next to my father's bed, wrapped in a scarf and longing for a warm shoulder to collapse onto. For someone else to come in and take charge.

My dad must have been nearing the end, which was why I was still there, gripped by a sense of duty that compelled me to stay until it happened. But I was desperate for sleep. I asked the nurse whether she thought I could go home for a few hours. I needed her permission to leave, so that I wasn't the daughter who abandoned her father in death as well as life.

'You look exhausted all on your own in there! Go and curl up and come back in the morning,' she suggested.

Hall pass given, I climbed into a cab and embarked on the now strangely familiar Magic FM ride from hospital to home.

I was making my way into the ward the next day when I got a text from my father's girlfriend.

> Dad died this am. He on ward til you get there. If I do not see you please contact me urgent – have documents you will need.

I looked at my dad's face for the final time. The white wiry brows, his mouth in the elegant repose of stillness, his parting swept slightly to the right, eternally in dashing Seventies TV presenter style.

'I'm sorry that we never straightened things out. But I really did love you. Say hello to Mum and Rach,' I said.

I left the hospital and stepped into the noise of the traffic-congested Euston Road. It felt surreal, losing the last thread of my past. Everyone had gone home, the lights had come on and it was just me with a bunch of memories. It was almost predictable that they had all ended up going in the wrong order, abandoning the traditional form of oldest goes first. We never had mastered the art of doing things by the rules.

I didn't tell anyone over the coming months how much my dad's death had impacted me. I didn't feel I had the right to feel sad about it. Nor did I talk about the weird feelings I was having, that the loss of my three family members in as many years had acted as a catalyst and hurled up things that felt overwhelming.

My weekly hour with Sue became a cocoon of comfort. It was like getting into a warm bath, where I could turn off the outside world and shed my skin. I remembered, when I collapsed at work after my mother died, that someone had said to me, 'But you're spending all this money on therapy, how could this happen? She's meant to be curing you!' I'd felt oddly envious of that worldview, where loss was dealt with in a neat time frame. 'Get fixed in twenty-eight days or your money back!'

I found myself calling the Samaritans some nights, just to talk to someone when the pain got bad and I felt out of control and didn't want to pretend anymore. I didn't tell any of my friends or even Sue how I was feeling. What if a policeman turned up and sectioned me? What if they put me on suicide watch or I was whisked off to one of those stately homes where the grandeur had been diluted by institutional fire doors, and I never came back?

And then one day I decided to make a phone call. And it changed everything.

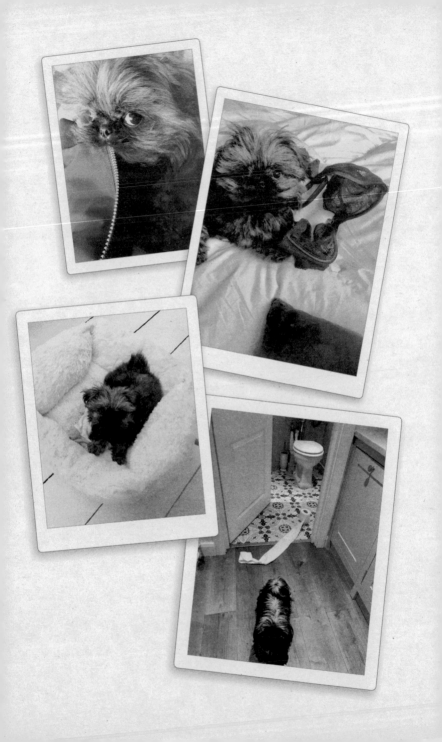

Part Three

Raymond

Chapter Twelve

October 2016

I handed over my phone, iPad, laptop and book. The woman took them from me and placed them in ziplock bags, writing my name on a label that she stuck firmly on the front. 'Is that everything?' she asked kindly, but with a tone suggesting this wasn't her first time at the contraband rodeo.

I nodded firmly. 'That's the lot.'

A few hours later I was standing in a room with sixteen people who were total strangers this morning. I had a sticker on my jumper announcing who I was. But in place of my name, I had written the word 'UNLOVEABLE' in black Sharpie. As first impressions went, it needed workshopping. Though some of the stickers on the assembled jumpers and T-shirts revealed even more challenging things about the wearer.

It might have looked like the world's most ineffective speed-dating event but it's called the Hoffman Process, a seven-day retreat that many people who've done talk about evangelically as something that has transformed their life.

I'd come across it occasionally over the years. A friend's boyfriend had done it, to confront a spiralling music-industry lifestyle. A comic I knew had signed up to address some unresolved issues with his late father and embrace his professional dreams. A celebrated foreign correspondent had written a moving piece about how it helped to shed the negative behaviours she feared passing on to her child.

I'd mentally filed it away as one of those things I might do in another, bolder life, along with leaving my office job and pursuing a career I felt passionate about. And redecorating my home. Oh, and finally getting a dog.

But I found all sorts of reasons not to do it. It cost too much money. People would take the piss out of me. Perhaps it was a scam run by narcissistic gurus who would make me walk on hot coals. And then deny me medical treatment for my third-degree burns because I had to 'really *feel* the power of that pain!'

My father had always hated this kind of self-exploration. He called it 'facile Californianism' and insisted it was all a symptom of 'the Me Decade'. So at the heart of my hesitance was also an inherited cultural snobbery. I was urban and sharp-tongued. I didn't belong with people who went on retreats. It all sounded very frayed friendship bracelets, inspirational quotes and earrings that balanced your chakras.

But for some reason I kept coming back to the Hoffman Process. One night I was up late, Googling cheery stuff like 'how to cope when your whole family suddenly dies'. I came across a piece written by a woman whose sister had been murdered. She had found the process helpful in confronting her lifelong anger over the loss. I found more reviews, one from the musician Goldie, who simply said 'it saved my life' and another by the actor Thandie Newton, who called it 'an MOT for the soul'. Even the respected psychologist Oliver James seemed happy to recommend it, suggesting that it helped strip away 'the layers of scar tissue created by past experiences.'

The process itself was shrouded in mystery. 'Graduates' (I imagined barefoot people accepting scrolls from a bearded man in a saffron tunic and beads) seemed reluctant to reveal a detailed breakdown of the course. I Googled 'Hoffman bad review' in order to confirm my worst fears. But oddly, people's experiences all seemed to follow a similar trajectory: they started out cynical, it was emotionally exacting, but they all came out of it a little lighter.

I'd chosen to come off my anti-depressants some months ago. I felt the meds had served their purpose, to get me functioning again. And I felt my issues with depression were more circumstantial than clinical.

But the bereavements had acted as an unwelcome truth-teller, forcing me to face something that I'd never had the courage to properly confront: a sense that I had lived my whole life as an adjunct to the people around me. Without my father around to be angry at, without my mother to deliver my script, without Rach to tell me what to do, I was kind of lost.

At times I felt swindled by their sudden collective disappearance, as if they'd extended an invitation to a non-stop drama that left other families in the shade, without warning me that the finale ended in mass carnage. I was the lone survivor in our very own *Game of Thrones* box set, which, just like that show, had malevolently decided to kill off one of the best-loved characters first.

I sounded Sue out about the Hoffman Process. 'I mean, it's not like the proper therapy I do here. It might be a disaster!' I said, worried she might not approve.

'If you want to do it, I think you should,' Sue replied. 'It's your decision, though, and one that only you can make.'

The following week I found myself at work, ignoring the feature on 'FIVE HOT Party Looks!' that had to be edited and going back to the Hoffman Process website. Again. I looked through the FAQs, which explained that they screen candidates to check they're in the right frame of mind. 'A few places remaining for our October course in Ireland!' a banner on the home page blinked, in welcoming orange font.

An hour later I was standing on the South Bank during my lunch break. I decided to call the Hoffman number. A party of schoolchildren were posing noisily for selfies by the Thames. A couple were emerging from the Mondrian hotel, huddling into each other against the cold. Students with bold trainer choices were chatting animatedly on their way into a sushi chain.

'I feel like I'm kind of watching other people live their lives. While I just get through the days,' I found myself saying to the male stranger on the other end of the line. 'Plus, I've had a lot of bereavements. My whole family in fact,' I said, slightly defensively. Keen to distance myself from the 'bored wanker with too much time and money on her hands' label.

'I see, I see,' the stranger said soothingly. 'Well, let's have a chat about the process. And you can have a think. But it sounds like we might be able to help you, Emily.'

I stroked my 'UNLOVEABLE' sticker, then glanced around the room at the sixteen other white labels listing everyone's 'word', the thing they most feared people finding out about them. I knew mine now, thanks to Sue. Embarrassingly, I didn't even have to pause when we were asked to select one. I couldn't tell you my credit card pin number. It had taken me a university degree course to understand the difference between the words 'naked' and 'nude'. But I was all over my own damage.

I first encountered some of the others at the airport. We smiled nervously as we boarded a coach to a remote house a few hours from Dublin. The introductions were made with the jittery bonhomie of contestants entering the *Big Brother* house. 'What the hell have we signed up for?' 'I'll DIE without my phone!'

There was a handsome man with Emirates first class luggage tags in expensive leisurewear exuding alpha maleness, who barely took his headphones off for the entire journey. I decided he was exactly the sort of bloke I hated. Arrogant and entitled. I nicknamed him the Crown Prince because of his imperial bearing. There was another man, introverted, happy to let the rest of the group take control of pleasantries. I immediately felt drawn to his less challenging aura. I chatted to a girl with messy blonde hair and a Lycra top, who looked like a yoga teacher.

She seemed sweet and vulnerable. I decided she would be my friend and named her Boho Gal. Another friendly woman joined our group, buttery highlights, fitted blazer and snowy dentistry. I christened her Belgravia Blonde.

We met the others when we arrived at the slightly careworn house at the bottom of a drive, set in pretty gardens. I looked at them all, wondering what secrets they carried and why they had decided to take this drastic step. I was introduced to the two women I was sharing an annexed wood cabin with: an elegant-looking forty-something with an ash blonde bob, and a warm matriarchal type with an infectious giggle. We were deferential with one other as we unpacked, offering the loan of shower gels as we organised our possessions, like nervous boarding-school freshers. But the small talk that oils most first encounters was curiously absent. We'd been advised not to discuss the facts of our lives outside of here. All that window dressing was to be stripped away over the next eight days.

We met our team leaders. J was a white-haired, academically dishevelled man exuding wisdom and disciplined thinking. M had the grace of a retired ballerina and the engaging warmth of Glinda the good witch in *The Wizard of Oz*. Which was appropriate because we were definitely not in lands I knew how to navigate anymore, Toto.

One of the first difficult lessons I had to learn was to stop using the word 'you' and commit to saying 'I'. When people talked about themselves in the group sessions (we didn't call them therapy), our collective dependency on the distancing tic of 'you' became astonishingly apparent.

'Then *you* feel . . .'

'And *you* think . . .'

J interjected patiently each time. 'You mean, "*I* feel." "*I* think"?'

He told us that every time we used the word 'you' instead of 'I', it minimised our experience and subtly projected it onto someone else. The more we used 'you', the more our opinions and feelings were handed over to another person. It was a way of relinquishing responsibility.

It seemed a bit weird at first, this endless grammar pedantry. I felt like saying, 'You can't be expected to police your language all the time. It's fucking ridiculous.'

But I didn't. Because J would have said, 'How about, "*I*" can't be expected to police "*my*" language all the time. It's fucking ridiculous?'

After a while it did start to feel strangely liberating committing to 'I'. Like choosing to leave a thick, ridged bootprint on the moment rather than my usual brush of a flip-flop. It was the verbal equivalent of coming straight to the point in emails, rather than using self-diminishing softeners like, 'I just wondered' or 'Does that make sense?'

I also began to see how much I needed to win a room – be the funniest, the most memorable. The first few irreverent heckles I made to gain the others' admiration were greeted with the polite tolerance given to an over-needy support act. My 'Look-at-me! Love me! Give me attention!' shtick fell a little flat in this room full of people who were there to turn their lives around.

I had sent over several pages' worth of information about

myself before I came, answering questions that started out fairly easily – 'What do you hope to gain from this?' – before descending into more hard-core areas like, 'What emotions are you afraid to express?' I had to pick out a list of qualities I recognised in each of my parents. Happy to oblige. But then they went and ruined it by asking me to pick out the ones I also recognised in myself. '*Hello*, that's the point? I'm not like either of them!' I almost shouted at the stupid questionnaire. Until I reluctantly found one. And another. It turned out there were absolutely shitloads of behaviour patterns I had in common with my parents.

This is the essence of the Hoffman Process: the idea that we pick up negative patterns in childhood and carry them throughout our lives, without realising it. Or as Philip Larkin put it slightly more eloquently, 'Man hands on misery to man. It deepens like a coastal shelf.'

It's a fairly simple theory, though the effects it describes are not always easy to see in your own life. But let's say you grew up around a lot of uncontrolled anger. You'll generally do one of two things. Grab the fury baton yourself and spend your whole life erupting at everyone, or quietly rebel by burying your real feelings.

The point is, mostly these are not unique qualities you're stuck with (mental health conditions aside). They're learned behavioural patterns, like a really disappointing inheritance. As Larkin also had it, 'They fill you with the faults they had and add some extra, just for you.' Whether we like it or not, children are hardwired to absorb the behaviours and moods of caregivers, for the simple reason that they need to survive. Just as dogs learn to hold out a paw, not because it's their funny little signature move, but because we give them attention every time they do it.

We had received work folders that bulged dauntingly with pages to be filled over the following week. We started off gradually, sharing our stories as we sat facing one another in a U shape. I heard about violent childhoods, divorce, death and alcoholism. Some people cried, some just recited their history, inured to its impact. Some wouldn't reveal until the very final day what had really sent them here.

'In the last three years all my family died,' I heard myself saying. My story sounded raw and unequivocal without the diversionary context of a conversation. Talking about each death without interruption, I realised that I had never had time to confront the impact of the individual losses. My family had become three trunks of trauma that I'd dumped in a cupboard, all piled on top of one another.

The Hoffman began to feel like the hero's quest in a movie. We had to battle the dark side in order to reach the celebratory *Star-Wars*-style victory ceremony at the end. We were going to have to confront our worst fear – our very own 'I am your father, Luke!' Darth Vader moment.

Much of our time was devoted to expelling the past through letters to our parents that we would never send – in my case that I could never send. The idea was to acknowledge how our negative patterns of behaviour had impacted our lives. I found myself writing with a manic confessional urgency, as if I'd opted for a cocktail called 'Our famous Speed and Truth Serum slammer!' But for every negative outpouring there was also a positive one. It was not about wallowing in self-pity; it was about learning.

The prospect of extended silent periods was the thing that filled me with most horror. I had always been terrified of silence, treating it as something to be stood up to, like a poisonous bully. Colleagues reached for headphones to block out my incessant chatter, receptionists in spas whispered, 'Sorry, we try to keep the noise to a minimum here.' I reacted to libraries like the Antichrist being led into a church.

The silence was announced by J in a firm, paternal tone. Sometimes it lasted for a couple of hours, sometimes until the next day. It felt almost funereal at first, as we sat in the kitchen's conservatory on faded floral couches sipping tea. The ticking clock, stirring of spoons on ceramic and crunching of biscuits was a clattering focus rather than a harmless backdrop.

I started to think about why I loathed silence. I realised that it was an entirely foreign phenomenon in our house. The only time I experienced it was when we had done something really, really bad. Our worst misdeeds were met by our mum not with hysteria, but with what Rach called 'the monk's vow'. Sometimes these silent treatments lasted for several days. They got more frequent as we got older. One of the longest came after a teenage ball. As Rach and I clambered out of Mum's car with our dates, in a whirl of floral scent and excitement, I caught sight of her face at the steering wheel, flooded with hurt. She didn't speak to us properly for weeks, walking out of the room when we came in and pinning notes on cupboards to communicate basic information.

She eventually revealed the reason behind the long Benedictine blackout.

'You didn't thank me properly for giving you a lift when you got out of the car,' she said. 'And I found it very hard to forgive.'

This became a long-standing joke between Rach and me. Lift-gate. But examining this cold case now, I think of what must have been rearing up in my mother's mind as we tumbled off into the night with our glitzy make-up and handsome escorts. That we didn't need her anymore. That we had the opportunity of youth and the excitement of futures. That she felt suddenly relegated to the role of elderly chauffeur, rather than the third member of our girlish triumvirate. Perhaps she just felt very alone.

Silence allows you to avoid the potential rejection that the truth risks. My grandmother often talked about my mother's 'terrible sulks' as a child. I now saw that they might have been a silent rebellion against the tornado of drunken madness she was flung into on a daily basis.

I gradually accepted that this was a pattern of punishment I had used myself occasionally, freezing out friends who had upset me rather than confronting them, sitting on boyfriends' texts for several hours to punish them. 'Look, which part of "Man hands on misery to man" did you not understand?' the spirit of Philip Larkin muttered impatiently as I finally made this behavioural link.

As the week passed I started to form strong bonds with everyone here, despite knowing so little about their lives outside. Or was it because of that? I knew the deep fears that kept the lawyer up at night, but I didn't know where he hung out or who his friends were. I had no idea what the young girl with the engaging manner studied at university or where she lived but I had an intimate knowledge of her childhood story.

'It's so strange meeting people's insides before their outsides,' I told M one day in our morning check-in. 'When you know what people hide, it's weird how much more compassion you have for them.'

I had heard the word 'transference' before, as a kind of therapy buzzword. I knew it was something to do with redirecting feelings from our past onto someone in our present. I had even thrown it into conversations when I was slagging someone off. But I'd never considered how I might be guilty of it. Pretty much on a daily basis.

That time when a boss closed their office door slightly too emphatically and glanced through the glass in my direction while talking to a colleague . . . Not sure how your thoughts go, but my internal story arc has always run like this. *They are talking about me. They have discovered something bad I did. They hate me. Why are they looking at that computer screen? Finalising the details of the termination letter, probably. Maybe I should just leave before they do it. Thank God for this unique insight I have that allows me to always know exactly what people are thinking. It is such a helpful tool that improves my life in every way.*

I won't even tell you where things went when a boyfriend started taking his phone into the bathroom except to say that it involved an apologetic private detective handing me photos in a manila envelope. (I'm not sure why the detective hadn't caught up with the digital age yet; it must have caused him a lot of issues.) 'No charge, Miss,' I imagined him saying. 'After seeing *those* photos, this one's on the house.'

You get the point. This was all what my father used to call 'emotion in wild excess of the fact.' None of it had anything to do with the boss or the boyfriend. It was more likely rooted in something that happened when I was eight years old, which I'd stored away, accessing it every time I felt vulnerable and adding another layer of paranoia. Until eventually it turned into a giant Jenga tower of toxic shame, which came crashing down with hurt fury when someone I ran into at a party forgot they'd met me before.

This noisy traffic from the past that runs through people's minds can become a bottleneck of fear. Psychologists refer to it when world-class strikers freeze in the face of a penalty shoot-out. Therapists explain that it's why people abandon relationships at the first sign of conflict. And why they erupt at a family Christmas when a relative suggests how to deal with a grouchy child.

We can't stop ourselves from feeling those triggers. But when we trace where they come from and confront the source, it becomes easier to understand our reactions. A bit like when Gareth Southgate made the England team sit through footage of previous penalty shoot-out disasters. You need to face the fuck-ups to stop being haunted by them.

There was one part of the Hoffman I had been really dreading. I'd read about it in an article before coming here. It's where you tell the other members of the group about the negative responses you had to them. I reside permanently on the corner of Love Me Street and People Please Avenue – I'd rather set fire to my eyebrows than give anyone a cast-iron reason not to like me. But it was explained to us that the purpose was to consider our own responses. How you experience someone is not always who they are. Still, I hoped no one was about to call me 'a mean selfish bitch with bad skin'.

I filled out my shit list of incidents and took a deep breath as I addressed the Crown Prince. He had become one of my closest pals over this week. It had been nice knowing him.

'When I first saw you at the airport I experienced you as being aloof with me, and arrogant. Freezing me out. When you put on headphones I took it personally as a rejection.'

He smiled, which seemed incredibly generous, considering.

I explained why I thought I'd reacted like that, how it echoed things I'd felt since childhood.

'How do you view him now, Emily?' asked M.

I gave the Crown Prince the spoiler alert of a grin so that he knew we were safely out of crap alley.

'He's probably one of the most honest people I've ever met. He's sensitive and kind. You know those people who make you happy when they walk in the room? That's how I feel about him.'

The unapologetically male Crown Prince must have had something in his eye, because he stoically wiped away a bit of moisture.

I did a similar thing with the Belgravia Blonde, who had become a close confidante, the lawyer who gave me a daily stomach ache from laughing. And the wary introvert from the airport, who was in fact a super smart and intuitive person underneath that label I'd initially slapped on him.

Then I braced myself for the onslaught of reactions people had initially had to me. Don't worry, I got mine all right.

'Very overly analytical.'

'Really not in a good place.'

'Intimidating and hostile.'

'Incredibly serious.'

'A sad darkness.'

'Putting on a front.'

'Judging everyone.'

At least trolls had the good manners to hide behind an egg avatar.

But somehow I didn't take any of it personally. You don't when someone owns their own messed-up reactions. And if I was really honest, some of it was true. That probably *was* how I'd come across, strapped into the fake armour I wore when I felt vulnerable. They had simply been responding to the false me. Who, it turned out, was a bit of a dick.

The group listed qualities they associated with the me they had got to know more intimately. They weren't words I thought anyone would have reached for before. Someone called me 'unafraid and honest'. Another said I was wise. I even got kind. But the Crown Prince used the word I never thought I'd hear. 'Loveable!' he said, and smiled.

It was a shit sandwich that was incredibly powerful. I don't advise you do it outside of a controlled setting, by the way. Telling the Ocado man that you experienced him as 'hostile, unhelpful and dismissive – a bit like my mother' will probably get you reported for customer abuse. But I could see that asking myself why I responded in a heightened way to certain situations was something that could be useful in my day-to-day life. And that mostly? It had absolutely nothing to do with anyone but me.

'But what if someone genuinely IS being a prick, J?' asked one of our troupe. 'Sometimes people just behave badly no matter how reasonable you are.'

'That's true of course. But you don't have the power to change their behaviour. You can control how you choose to respond, though.'

It wasn't all joyful warm moments. There were some tough ones, where I started to question the whole process. We were doing an exercise about forgiveness, trying to feel compassion for our parents, when I felt a hot fury descend on me. I was angry at the thought of others walking out of here, able to potentially heal the past with actions. What was I meant to do, have a cosy chat over a bunch of tombstones? I stormed out as we finished and started to cry in a corridor. The Crown Prince rushed over and asked someone to quickly fetch J.

I hadn't cried this violently since I was a child.

'I can't make my peace with my dad. He's not here, J. Do you not get it? It's too late.'

'But what if there was a way to make your own peace, Emily? Forgiveness comes from within. I think it's possible.'

The evening after my mini-meltdown I wrote a letter to my father and felt immediately lifted. I told him that I now understood why he kept running away. That I knew he had been frightened. And that it had felt easier to keep hunting out fresh starts than to confront the mess inside that always made him leave. I thanked him for our best bits – his wit, his brilliant mind, his wise insight and his refusal to conform – the things that I'd benefited from, rather than the things I never got.

And it turned out that J was right. You really don't have to have someone standing in front of you in order to forgive them.

One of the final things we did was to talk about our future and the life we wanted. I knew what I wanted. Things that I had always felt belonged to the others. Things that involved, to borrow Frank's phrase, doing to the world rather than letting the world do to me. I made a list.

1. A beautiful space to live in, a home filled with things I love. One that reflects my weird passions, rather than stuff I've seen in interiors magazines. My brief to myself is 'French farmhouse meets spoilt child star bedroom, with a hint of *What Ever Happened to Baby Jane* chic.'

And I'm going to buy that lamp that someone in fashion told me was a bit 'two years ago'.

2. A new career devoted to doing what I love – writing things I feel passionate about and radio presenting. I want to interview people not in hotel rooms for half an hour about perfume while a publicist glares at me, but chatting to them honestly about their lives. And I am

going to write a book. Not tell people I'm writing a book while I look at YouTube videos of reality shows – but actually commit to writing the sodding thing.

3. I am going to get a puppy.

No really. I'm going to get a puppy.

Chapter Thirteen

Three months later

'What are you going to call him?' asked Mimi from the passenger seat, juggling our live chat with WhatsApp conversations, which I suspected had liberal uses of the crying-laughing emoji.

We were driving down to Hampshire to meet some Shih Tzu puppies.

'I'd kind of like an old pub regular's name, like Derek or Harry.'

'Or Raymond?' she replied.

'Raymond! Then we could nickname him Ray.' Ray had been Rach's nickname. 'I really love that idea.'

'Ohmigod, you HAVE to call him Raymond!'

She had been choosing music from my phone and we'd been singing along to Taylor Swift and Katy Perry. Shortly after our Raymond revelation she settled on a Spice Girls greatest hits album. The ballad 'Mama' came on, and I sang along, even though I had always been more drawn to their leather-clad desert ninjas phase, when they moaned about boys throwing 'far too much emotions' their way.

Maybe it was because I was listening to a song called 'Mama' with Mimi. Maybe it was just the power of cheap pop music bringing back memories of applying Nineties lip liner in bar toilets with my sister. But Emma Bunton's sugary voice managed to break me.

'Well, this is awkward, I'm crying at the *actual* Spice Girls,' I laughed, adopting Mimi's vernacular to make the moment less awks for her. I noticed that she'd briefly abandoned her phone, and was looking at the countryside whizzing past, wiping her own tears away.

'I think it's kind of nice when we remember her like this,' I said, reaching for Mimi's hand. 'Like we're being honest that we still miss her. And how much she'll always mean to us.'

She wiped her nose on her sleeve. 'Yeah, I know. She'd be so happy you're getting a dog Em.'

'I think she would. And I love that you're coming with me to find one. Because I really think that would have made her even happier.'

It had been less than four months since I got back from the Hoffman Process.

It had felt quite odd re-entering the world after those eight days of seclusion. I'd booked into a Dublin hotel for a couple of nights as a kind of half-way house, something that was recommended to help reintegrate ourselves back into the noise of everyday life. 'You can land with quite a bump!' we were told. 'Rest, eat well and try to spend some time on your own reflecting.'

Waking up in the hotel the first morning, I felt different. I hadn't rushed to drown out my solitude by scrolling through Twitter, or sending texts. I'd just sipped my tea and sat with my own thoughts for a bit. It felt very grown up, like a heroine in a French film. I'd had the same feeling when I wandered through Dublin, abandoning the instinctive urge to check out clothes in the department store filled with noisy crowds. I'd popped over to the park instead, to go for a walk. I had never just gone for a walk before. What kind of freak did that? My kind of freak, now.

The next day I'd spotted a jewellery shop. I remembered Jane once telling me that she bought herself a piece of jewellery every time she successfully completed a movie script. I had written a new script in a way, I decided.

'Can I see that bracelet, please?' I said to the friendly shop assistant with fuchsia hair.

It was rose gold and raised like a bridge. It was perfect.

'Do you want anything inscribed on it?' asked Fuchsia Hair.

There were two words I was thinking about. They were not words I would have chosen a week ago. I would have worried about smart, literary people thinking they were sentimental or 'self-help book, a bit "basic bitch".' I would probably have said those very things myself. I didn't now. I wanted to inscribe the bracelet with something that felt right – not something that looked right.

'Love and Truth,' I said, resisting the urge to apologise for my route one, gap-year tattoo choice.

'That's so lovely!' said Fuchsia Hair approvingly.

She handed it over when it was done and I admired it on my wrist.

Truth was something I was getting more comfortable with – we were still struggling through those awkward first dates, slowly getting acquainted. But I was going to try and treat it like a keeper rather than a brief fling.

Love had undergone a bit of an extreme makeover for me. It was now nothing like my old view of it – as something you showed off to the world, that made you feel validated and romantically desired. I was starting to see it as something you gave out rather than a thing you acquired, spread among everyone you cared about, not a goal to seize and win for yourself.

I'd also realised that there was a basic requirement for love that there was no way round – you had to risk being unloveable to get it back from anyone.

I had never really got how love could co-exist with flaws before. I had begun to assume that feeling insecure or in need of re-assurance made you defective. And I was drawn to dynamics where that message would be reinforced. I thought voicing your doubts and fears and anger, as a woman, always ended with you being dismissed as 'fucking mad, mate!', the high-maintenance, psycho bullet someone had dodged. I hadn't known it was okay to express those feelings. And that not feeling free to express them was an issue you shouldn't ignore. I hadn't known you could find a way to do it calmly and directly, without lugging an entire baggage hall into the room.

I hadn't known that you could accept how you had once felt as a child, but that those feelings didn't need to get erected as stone tablets that could never be rewritten. That it was okay to see my parents as flawed and it didn't make me weak to still feel love for them. One of the most powerful lessons I learned on the Hoffman Process was contained in just eight small words.

'Everyone is guilty – no one is to blame.'

And the minute I reminded myself of that, it was hard to stay pissed off at anyone for too long.

My Hoffman friends and I communicated regularly, via our WhatsApp group. We referred to ourselves as 'The Geese', flying separately but supporting one another, always there if someone was having a moment.

My friends at home noticed a change in me as soon as I got back. 'How the fuck has it changed your skin?' said Polly. 'You're so much calmer,' said Cathy. 'You seem different, kind of serene,' said a friend of the Rosses, James. 'I'm not saying you weren't before,' he rushed to reassure me. But he didn't need to. It was true; no one would ever have used that word to describe me.

Sue was happy to see how much I'd benefited from the Hoffman Process. But mostly she was proud of me for having taken the decision to go. Leaving the bootprint on the world for once, not the flip-flop. And we kept up our regular sessions. We weren't yet quite at the sign saying, 'You are leaving bear country.'

I was aware that the newly evangelised, like the suddenly sober or the recent convert to exercise, could be really fucking annoying. Or those new parents who tell people, 'Honestly, you don't know what love is until you have a child.' (Rach's recommended response to this, by the way, was always, 'Does that include Fred West?') So I watched myself. I tried not to be one of those idiots who offer unsolicited advice. 'Perhaps, as a child you witnessed your father's anger and it scared you?' is after all quite a punchable thing to say to someone who just wants to offload about a marital row.

It was impossible to maintain the tranquil outlook constantly. I slipped up, lapsed into old patterns and habits, had bad days and even bad weeks. But it was a bit like those song lyrics you learned off by heart when you were a teenager – they're stored away in the back of your mind, and sometimes you just recall them automatically, without even trying.

Within weeks of returning home I discovered that my magazine had been a victim of the economy and was moving online. I was offered the chance to take a pay-off, and I grabbed it.

A month or so later I was chatting to Polly over coffee. 'By the way, there's an executive at *The Times* who does all their podcasts and loves your radio show. Maybe you should talk?' she said.

There was a time when I would have absorbed that brief hit of praise but not acted on it. What if he was just being polite? Maybe he meant someone else? But this time I decided to be proactive. I sent him an email. I wanted to suggest hosting an interview-based podcast for *The Times*.

When we met he said, 'I don't know what you think of this . . . but I wondered if you could do it over a dog walk. Are you a fan of dogs?'

The Times asked me to write a feature to launch the new show. I prepared to write the sort of piece I'd always written. A sunny, joke-littered, 'aren't dogs the absolute best?' type of thing. But I couldn't write that anymore. Instead I poured out the truth. About losing Rach and my parents in just three years, about the emotions it had thrown up and the Hoffman Process. I wrote about Giggle and the way he'd helped with loss, and about my decision to finally get a dog. I ended the piece not with a wry aside but with something Hugh Laurie once said in an interview that had stayed with me. 'There is no such thing as ready – there is only now.'

It felt frightening spilling out my guts for the judgment of strangers. I had never revealed this much truth to anyone before. The comments started piling up on my Twitter page; people were sharing stories of dogs that had helped them through tough times. Hundreds of pictures of Labradors with tongues hanging out, dozing terriers, excitable poodles and every mixed breed imaginable. Staffies that kept people going through depression, border collies who comforted families through cancer, rescue dogs inherited from lost loved ones. Or people simply urging me to make good on my promise of getting my own dog, tempting me with pictures of puppies, saying, 'Ruby and Spike welcome you to the world of dog people!'

People's kindness stunned me. I realised that you could devote your life to being the one with all the answers, to looking cool and funny and sharp and sorted. You could reach for the smartarse over the honest. Be spiky and unyielding instead of raw and scared. But the only thing that ever really connected you with anyone else was the truth.

'Well, you'd better get a bloody dog now, after that piece,' texted one friend. 'Are you absolutely sure? They're an awfully big responsibility,' said another, until I reminded them that they had several children. 'Whatever you do, avoid sausage dogs – the vets bills are terrible!' advised someone else.

I decided not to listen to what anyone else thought. When I met him, I would know.

'We've got some super boys and girls,' said Theresa, the friendly middle-aged lady who was ushering Mimi and me through the gate leading to her Hampshire house, decorated with brightly coloured hanging baskets. We were hit by a cacophony of barking. She went off to fetch tea and the wriggling litter of new arrivals, who were all in the running to be, if not exactly America's next top model, *then at the very least* Britain's most spoilt dog.

I had spent several weeks researching my puppy with the tireless dedication of someone scrolling through an ex's Facebook page. And I had decided three things.

It could do with being on the petite side. I couldn't really picture a Great Dane navigating its giant paws around my bijou home. I flashed forward to it crashing over lamps and struggling to wedge its vast frame round my cottagey wooden stairs. So it was a no from me. Even if their reputation as affectionate couch potatoes did fit my likes column.

Compatibility was something we needed to establish from the off. A dog whose dating profile would read, 'Adventurer! Marathon runner! Just back from hiking round the Lake District!' was not going to work well in my world. The listing I was looking for was, 'LOVE cosy nights in, cuddling on the sofa and major LOLZ. Prefer pooing during scheduled walks to dumps on the kitchen floor.'

I wanted a dog that was silly and slightly strange-looking

rather than sleek and polite. One with a ridiculous face that made me laugh, and a weird personality – the kind that would have totally got my family. And I wanted to avoid any dog with what Sue calls 'an avoidant attachment style'. Though perhaps I wouldn't mention that to the nice lady in Hampshire.

I had done endless online quizzes about the right dog for me, answering questions like 'how do you react when another driver cuts you off?' (Assume immediate guilt.) 'What do you do when a friend tells you a story you've heard many times before?' (Nod but hurry them along.) These responses, for reasons that still remain a mystery, paired me with a toy poodle.

The various rehoming charities brought up pictures of sweetly vulnerable whippets and various mixed breeds. There was a lovely terrier called Ricky who was ten years old. But I decided that taking in a dog in the mid or closing stages of his life was not something I was up to quite yet. I needed a companion at the very start of his journey.

There was a website I began to obsess over, a sort of TripAdvisor for dog breeds, with no-nonsense reviews highlighting traits like rowdiness, bad breath and, more alarmingly, 'legal liabilities'. I avoided the world of doggy electronic ankle tags and investigated the Pomeranian, looking under the cutesy heading 'What's good about 'em, what's bad about 'em . . .'

'The typical Pomeranian thinks he's hot stuff,' the character profile began. Pomeranians were apparently vivacious and 'delightfully alive' (which was a bonus as I was all funeralled out for now), as well as being attentive and intelligent. But they wouldn't take orders from anyone they considered 'beneath them in importance'. I suddenly cut to a life based around him lying in stately splendour across my bed glaring at me, while I cowered below on a blow-up lilo.

Poodles and sausage dogs still had everything to play for, but my eye kept being drawn to the Ewok-resembling Shih Tzu. I discovered they were proud and sometimes arrogant but with 'a sweet-natured temperament – they like cuddling on laps and soft pillows.' It was only at the end that the devastating left hook was delivered. 'GREAT for senior citizens!'

My main Shih Tzu experience so far had been via the Rosses' adorable dog, Captain Jack, who had belonged to my eldest goddaughter, Betty. He had a sweet, gentle disposition that reflected hers. He would occasionally join the pack squabbles over a toy rubber chicken but was happiest snoozing across us devotedly, while we watched TV.

'They are *such* good-natured little things,' Jane told me, with the poorly concealed anticipation of a car dealer smelling the closing of a sale. She had been a voice of unwavering enthusiasm on my dog quest, mainly because she knew more than anyone how brilliant I was at finding excuses for not following through.

'Look, I just think it'd be the perfect dog for you. I mean, you could just go and see one . . .'

A few weeks later I met another Shih Tzu.

'Megan, Dalai, stop being dicks!' I heard from beyond the door of a pretty converted church. I was relived to discover that the 'dicks' were dogs rather than children. The Canadian comic, Katherine Ryan, ushered me in, all manga eyes and dazzling smile. I was interviewing her for my *Times* podcast and we chatted, walking round her local park with her three dogs,

Manny the Yorkie and the two dicks – Dalai the Tibetan terrier, and Megan the tiny black and white Shih Tzu.

'Megan don't EAT POO! That's GROSS,' she yelled as the dogs sprinted around the park with a confident street smarts that sat unexpectedly with their pocket-sized glamour. She told me about her life as a single mum raising Violet, and the village of female friends that acted as an extended family. We popped back to hers and I noticed all the framed family pictures – Violet in a pink feather boa and oversized sunglasses with her pals, a mother–daughter shot of them hugging on a sunny day. It felt like a dog family but built in a different way. There were no accountant dads in the frames or family estate cars in the drive. This life had nothing to do with those conventional beats of adulthood that had always felt out of my reach. I thought your story couldn't begin until you fell into the safety of another person's arms. But perhaps a dog family was something you could make yourself, in whatever way you liked.

Mimi and I were covered in a battalion of Shih Tzu puppies. Two snowy white little girls with half-closed eyes wriggled on our laps, their tongues scratching at our fingers.

'Now here's a special boy!' announced Theresa proudly, entering with the most peculiar-looking puppy I had ever seen. 'This is Biscotti!'

Biscotti's eyes darted about wildly, as if he was worried the police were about to appear and interrupt his street-corner transaction. He had slight shadowy markings under his eyes, the sort that would force you to say to a friend, 'Is everything okay at home?' His coat was cream with biscuity strands and a curiously fuzzy texture. It reminded me of a sheepskin rug I owned that was urgently in need of a dry clean.

'Hey Biscotti,' I coaxed and he responded with a human pensioner's croak, before assaulting the air with manic spins. He finally seized his teeth into a leather cushion, gnawing its decorative floral rosette hungrily.

'He's ever such a character is our Biscotti!' said Theresa and I smiled warmly, as you do when a parent indulges their hyperactive offspring.

Biscotti started to tug insistently on my trainer laces. He was the type whose friends insisted 'You'll LOVE him when you get to know his humour,' a charismatic outlier who would make life endlessly entertaining. I found myself drawn to his wild temperament.

'I think Biscotti is . . . a little bit crazy?' whispered Mimi.

'Maybe that's why I like him,' I admitted, as Biscotti launched himself at a sofa leg like it contained the spirit of Satan. 'But he is . . . a handful.'

I looked at the quietly obedient creamy puppies on our laps, the kind who would text to check you got home safely. I basically wanted Biscotti's spirited joy with their devoted tranquillity. A pattern of my lifelong modus operandi. *I'll have that charming, alpha boyfriend with a side order of commitment and loyalty. Give me the noisy ebullience of my family with the dependability of the Simpsons.* Always agonising over the way I wanted things to be was exactly how I'd ended up with a big handful of nothing.

Biscotti crashed into a table leg before attempting to liberate the innards of a urine-soaked puppy pad. I tried to remind myself of the golden mantra, 'Everyone is guilty, no one is to blame.' Even Biscotti.

'Oh, I forgot to show you this little love,' said Theresa, returning with a slightly gleeful smile. She placed a fluffy treacle-coloured cloud of fur on the floor. 'He doesn't have a name yet.'

The cloud of fluff waddled over to us, his tail twerking imperiously behind him. He looked up at me through ombre highlights, tiny pink tongue poking out, glossy brown eyes assessing me curiously. His front paw scratched briefly at the sofa leg and then stopped.

'He wants to come up, it's so sweet!' said Mimi.

I picked him up and buried my nose in his fur as he wriggled around my hands snuffling. He licked at my chin a few times before settling into my arms with a tiny sigh. He didn't look like a puppy. More like the result of a one-night stand between a Wookie and an Ewok, with his teddy-bear features, penetrating gaze and shaggy hair.

'It's funny, that one doesn't bark, he makes a little grunting sound,' said Theresa, as right on cue he let out a yawn that sounded like Chewbacca heralding an approaching Storm Trooper.

'I used to have a Chewbacca diary,' I told Mimi. 'I wrote all my entries to "Dear Chewie." Until Mum stole it after a fight and wrote "Dear Chewie, why am I so MEAN?" across all the pages.'

Mimi laughed and I stroked his tiny soft head.

'He's good as gold that one! Such a happy, loving little chap,' Theresa said. 'Not a bad bone in his body.'

I released him on to the floor and he wiggled over to the puppy pad, sniffing the edges before releasing a spot of yellow. He made his way back, placing his paws flat on the floor while poking his rear in the air, as if he was trying out a yoga pose for the first time. Then he rested his head on my trainers and fixed me with a devoted stare.

'He's my dream dog,' I said. Exactly what the experts advised against doing. Think about it before finally committing. Don't go for the first one who shows you attention. Visit several times. Assess behaviour for potential signs of conflict with other members of the litter. But he was simply the most vivacious and loving little thing I had ever seen. He made my heart burst.

'Can we meet his mum?' I asked, deciding to observe at least one rule. And hoping it went better than some of my previous meet-the-parent sessions. (One involved a boyfriend's father whispering to him, 'Don't use the Gordon's today please – get the Sainsbury's gin out of the cellar.')

Mimi and I went into the kitchen and I was introduced to a slightly larger, more worldly version of the Ewok puppy. She looked at me expectantly as I squatted down to offer her my hand. She gave it a lick, as if to say, *Yep, this passport seems to be in order*.

'I promise I will look after him for you! And he'll always be safe and loved,' I said.

She didn't respond – because dogs have a habit of not doing that. But I said it out loud anyway, confident that this was the kind of house where solemn vows to dogs weren't seen as potential mental health issues.

'FFS, it's just a dog,' would, by the way, not be an unreasonable response to reading this. I realise that dogs' hobbies don't extend much beyond, shitting, pissing, eating, begging and running. I know that Hitler loved dogs – so yes, I'm in great company. I also appreciate that getting a dog is not exactly some huge achievement. Homeless people with a range of massive practical problems still manage to look after their dogs. And I know that it's easy to love a dog because they don't answer back. I have no logical argument to rebut any of this. The very nature of keeping a dog is illogical. Dogs are here for a good time, a fairly basic time and crucially not a long time. You nurture them, structure your life around them and love them with all your soul, knowing that this story is destined to end in heartbreak and loss.

But I simply couldn't argue with how this little chap made me feel. Loving. And loveable. For once, I listened not to my fearful, rationalising adult voice but to my childish unspoilt heart.

Mimi and I went back into the living room. The Ewok waddled towards us and glanced up at me. 'You have to have him, Em,' Mimi said. 'You just have to.'

It's true what they say – when you know, you know.

'How soon can I bring him home?'

Chapter Fourteen

'Is he dead? Oh my God he's dead. I can't see him breathing.'
This was pretty much my running commentary (press the red button for paranoid hysteria) as I drove home to London with Ray a few weeks later. Honey, my youngest goddaughter, had come with me for the pick-up. 'But I have to be back at 3.00pm for my therapist, okay?' she told me, with the impressively uncomplicated candour of a Gen Z-er.

I was grateful to have her along as a comforting lap for Raymond on the journey back, as I lurched from one imagined catastrophe to another. Honey and I had developed a close friendship of our own now, the kind that transcends generations. And she came in handy when you needed to ask a question like 'How exactly do I "air drop" something?'

Honey reassured me that Raymond was definitely breathing. Which was a huge relief. If my friends had to hear about any more deaths on my watch, they'd probably react like that woman who went viral when she was once vox-popped on the news about the snap election. 'You're JO-KING. Not ANOTHER one?'

Raymond was curled up on his pink fluffy blanket inside his carrier on Honey's lap, head placed snugly on his tiny paws, adorable dreamy grunts filling the car as he drifted into REM sleep.

I decided to fill his dreams with exciting adventures – runs through wet grass, country excursions so he could leap in fields, neighbourhood strolls where he could christen every lamppost and dog dates with eligible males and females. (I already had a feeling Raymond ticked the LGBT box.)

'There is a big BUNCH of preparation to do for when your new fur baby comes home!' I had been advised by one American dog book. The book's daunting localisms filled me with panic. 'Make that *yard* doggy friendly!' Find ways to prevent 'puppy biting *Momma's pant* legs!' And find 'a RELIABLE doggy holistic practitioner for your *best bud*.'

I needed a yard? A yard sounded utilitarian and vast, the sort of thing men in baseball caps hosed down while listening to 'Sweet Home Alabama' as they cracked open a Coors. My 'yard' was a tiny concrete patio with some Nineties decorative pebbles and defunct fairy lights that foxes had chewed through. The kind of garden used for cigarette smoking in your twenties rather than the daily exercise space for a dog. And I would have loved to locate a 'RELIABLE doggy holistic practitioner' if I'd had any clue what that even meant.

Luckily there was a friendly woman in my local pet shop who helped me prepare for Ray's first days. I emerged with some of the 'basic essentials' . . .

1 'super soft' luxury doggy bed

1 ceramic blue food bowl

1 ceramic blue water bowl

2 packets of puppy pads

2 large bags of dry food

10 small pouches of wet food

2 bags of treats

1 box of cleansing 'banish gunk!' eye pads

1 bottle of blueberry-scented shampoo

1 tartan harness

2 leads

1 green Gonzo lookalike toy

1 fleece-lined car carrier

1 polka-dot carrying sling

1 tennis ball

1 rose gold poo-bag holder

100 poo bags

1 tube of fresh breath gel

1 packet of chewy dental twists

2 super soft blankets

1 puppy playpen with gate

1 brush and comb set

1 furry meerkat in a Santa outfit

Look, I never said I wasn't going to spoil him.

The first thing I did was turn the playpen into his own little bachelor pad, but instead of an Xbox and old pizza crusts I filled it with fluffy pink blankets and bowls of Evian water. (I know, a bit Kardashian.) The good news was dogs rarely soiled their own bedding area – only on occasions when they felt they had no other option. To be fair, I knew a bloke at university who was a bit like that.

But Ray's legs were too short. I'm not body-shaming him – they were genuinely too tiny for him to make it into his new pad. I improvised a makeshift step up to the puppy pen using three paperbacks – Cesar Millan's *How to Raise the Perfect Dog*, *The Life-Changing Magic of Tidying* by Marie Kondo and *Year of Yes* by Shonda Rhimes. I liked to think he would be inspired by the contents of all three.

Ray investigated his cosy new apartment, which I had placed next to my bed – ignoring his cries would make me feel like less of a sociopath if I was at least in the same room. He descended the paperback books warily and padded around the bedroom exploring plug sockets – 'No Ray!' – chewing the hairdryer cable – 'Stop it, Ray!' – and munching on something that his terracotta-stained grin later identified as Chanel bronzing powder. 'Jesus, RAAAY!'

I was basically sharing my living space with someone who had the experimental urges of a teenager at Glastonbury. I was in a constant state of high alert, convinced his first sneeze was a heart attack, worried about him tumbling down the stairs and terrified of eating chocolate in case he got toxic poisoning from licking up a crumb. I could already hear the vet gravely dictating the death certificate. 'Time of death – 2.00pm. Cause of death – Cadbury's Celebrations.'

But it was a fear tax I was willing to pay – because I was stupidly overwhelmed with love for this silly little thing. I watched him when he was snoring, resting his head on the tummy of his hippo toy, jabbing at an enemy with his paws as he dreamed. I laughed when he leapt around on my duvet before collapsing exhausted on his back, extending his soft belly to rub, rolling his eyes in bliss. Or when his bottom wiggled into the laundry cupboard and he emerged with a pink satin bra strap clenched in his jaw. Ray lifted sadness with his endless good-natured enthusiasm. He gave me a reason to wake up and face the day. He made me deliriously happy just by existing.

There was simply nothing I would change about him.

Until I discovered something called 'stubborn Shih Tzu syndrome'.

'Come on, Ray Ray! Come, walkies!'

I think it was Nietzsche who said, 'All truly great thoughts are conceived while walking.' Ray didn't agree with Nietzsche. He stared at me with cool disdain. Before lying on the floor, paws stretched out ahead of him, as immovable as a decorative stone lion.

I waved treats in his direction, squatted down on all fours to coax him, even stamped my feet frantically to demonstrate the excitement ahead. 'Ray Ray loves walkies!' But he was not about to be swayed. He was committed to a life behind closed doors.

This battle of wills continued for weeks. I begged; he resisted. I tugged the lead; he stiffened, threatening to drag himself on the pavement like Hector paraded through Troy behind Achilles's chariot.

'My dog won't walk?' I asked my friend the internet, throwing in 'Why is my Shih Tzu sulking with me?' I finally got in touch with a dog trainer for advice.

'Refusals often hide nerves,' she explained and suggested

propping a small piece of wood between my patio and the kitchen door, then placing several treats along the pirate ship plank. 'Make him think it's his idea.' I remembered Rach once telling me that that was the secret to a lasting relationship, so I figured it was worth a try. It took him at least fifteen minutes of deliberation to travel two feet down the ramp to the first treat.

'Do I have to do this every time?' I asked the dog trainer, appalled.

'Just be patient,' she said with a smile. 'There's no rush. Dogs respond well to calm encouragement, not panic and frustration.'

I wasn't known for my patience. I interrupted people, willing them to get to the point. I stifled screams when the person paying before me started asking questions about loyalty cards. I performed dramatic three-point turns in traffic. But I simply couldn't be intolerant with Ray. He was too vulnerable, too sweet, too basically decent for me to lose my temper with him. So he forced me to adopt some self-control over my slightly antsy style.

I tried to approach our walks with a slightly more 'Romantic poets' mindset – for their own sake rather than as a practical dash. No mobiles, no sighing, no angst.

'Oh, we're doing this,' I told him as he glowered at the lead. 'I'm not having you turning into one of those weirdo teenage sons who never leaves the house.'

We hadn't made it far before he adopted the stone lion pose. Sometimes he did full-on Superman-in-flight – paws stretched ahead, stomach welded to the pavement. I could be locked there for up to twenty minutes in a total stand-off, whispering gentle encouragement. People would burst out laughing when they saw us. 'Look at that woman's dog – he won't move!'

But eventually he started to experiment with wobbling down the street. His waterfall tail swished as he discovered the joys of leaves and approaching cockapoos. I was proud that my new managerial tactics had paid off, that I had swapped my archaic 'shouting from the technical area in an anorak' style for a more modern 'calmly offering support in tailored suits' approach.

Within a few weeks he was scampering with excitement as we approached the wrought-iron gates of Highgate's Waterlow Park, rushing towards poodles and St Bernards as I weighed up whether their owners were the 'hello, what's this boy called?' type or the 'Mortimer! Get away from there immediately!' variety.

'I had no idea that dog walking involved so much talking to strangers,' said the comic, Lee Mack, with comedic grumpiness, when he guested on my podcast. He wasn't a dog owner. You could tell this because when the dog we'd borrowed for the day did a poo, Lee's response was, 'Call the police.'

But I knew what he meant about the whole talking thing. It had taken me by surprise initially, too. I'd met a whole new crew since I'd been out walking Ray.

There was Jane the model booker who owned Willow the poodle. Like me, she was inclined towards the 'life's too short not to give your dog a blueberry facial' school of thought. Groups of girls wearing my old school uniform gathered round to cuddle Ray as I told them ye olde tales of calculators and boys calling you on landlines. There were familiar faces I nodded to, like the elderly couple with their own Shih Tzus, Minty and Salty. 'They're older so they're better behaved,' they informed me a bit haughtily. And the man who owned Cloud the Bichon Frisé. Cloud had been named after her hairdo, I assumed, a spectacularly fluffed out white bubble perm that made her look a bit like an astronaut's wife.

It was strange finding myself suddenly engaging with people in my own neighbourhood that I had probably walked past scores of times before, carrying the ingrained territorial hostility of a Londoner. Too cool and suspicious to talk to anyone outside of my heavily vetted social circle.

'Dogs can be transitional objects,' Sue told me when I recounted how grateful I'd been to have Ray with me recently when someone was being slightly spiky.

So I realised Ray was serving the purpose of that toy we clung to in childhood, the one that helped us cope with sleeping with the lights off.

Dogs perform that useful function for us a lot, socially (also, see babies), acting as diversions during tense family interactions, easing introductions, being used as pawns in rows: 'Daddy's loud shouty voice frightened you, DIDN'T IT?'

But dogs also help us to cast off our prickly defensiveness towards strangers. I'm biased, but I can honestly say that something about Ray's fluffiness and daft face inspired childlike joy. Businessmen's grimaces turned into grins, mums with screaming children fell gratefully upon his distracting cuteness. 'Look at the doggy, darling!' Groups of teenage boys broke off from their expletive-laden taunting of each other to say, 'That ain't even a dog, man, what is it even tho? Like *Star Wars* shit?'

Ray allowed me to see people at their most benign and nurturing – he was an antidote to anger. Even the man at the late-night shop down the road, who greeted the regular stream of loud drunken patrons with a guilty-till-proven-innocent suspicion, beamed when we walked in to buy Coke Zeros. 'I hate dogs. But this boy? This boy special,' he said, throwing a Calippo ice lolly into a bag gratis for him.

I felt grateful that Rach and I had both stayed in the area close to Holly Village even as adults. It was significant now, that connection to our past, in a way I never could have realised it would be.

Sometimes I strolled with Ray past the little hut near the park's tennis courts, remembering Rach and me sharing cigarettes with teenage boys. Or I'd take him for a wander down to the park's café, Lauderdale House, former home of King Charles II's mistress, Nell Gwynne. My dad had often told Rach and me stories about her when he walked us up to our primary school – his job after Mum announced that she didn't do walks (or mornings). He particularly liked to quote Nell's response when a baying crowd called her a Catholic whore. 'Pray, good people, be civil. I am the *Protestant* whore!' he would cry into the suburban morning air, as passing families narrowed their eyes in disapproval and Rach and I died with shame.

Ray and I passed the grassy slope that had acted as a makeshift toboggan run during snowy winters, where Rach would bravely descend the drop on a National Portrait Gallery tea tray. It had featured Holbein's Henry VIII, his face still just about visible beneath the red wine stains, fag burns and coffee rings.

I had sometimes felt a sting of pain when I visited this park the year before, after my family had all finally gone. Frustrated at the sense of a past without any surviving witnesses. But it felt different now that Ray was with me, the centre of the new world I had shaped for myself. As if I could dip into my family highlights rather than dwell in the dark moments of drama.

I had asked Sue why, even long before those losses, I had spent my whole life feeling inescapably swathed in gloom walking past any place that held memories.

She told me, 'You grew up thinking you weren't a person in your own right. That you were solely here to perform, to serve others. You didn't feel like you existed outside of your experiences. So when the experience is gone, it leaves a big hole inside.'

This made sense to me. When I was younger I had attempted to fill that hole with hedonistic nights out and fleeting encounters with men who became entertaining punchlines. I pretended I was giddy with the thrill of it all, serving up anecdotes about endless walks of shame in alien postcodes. I knew people who genuinely seemed able to throw themselves into these adventures, emerging unscathed from the experience. But I always felt sad and vulnerable afterwards. So I got through it all by buckling on my armour, made out of stolen traits from the kick-ass heroines I idolised. All perfectly admirable feminist role models – providing you took the bits you wanted and balanced them out with some sense of your own authentic character. It didn't occur to me that it was possible to be strong while admitting that sometimes you felt frightened. That you could say no, and call out bad behaviour and still be kind. That forgiveness didn't mean weakness. That you could have boundaries without being brittle. Love people for being imperfect. Be funny without being malicious. Live the life you wanted. That it was okay just to be you.

'I feel as though I'm slowly filling the hole up, Sue. Is it possible that one day it won't be there anymore?'

'We're getting there, Emily. I'm very proud of you. And Rachael would be, too. I know that.'

'I know this might be crossing a professional line – but am I allowed to hug you?'

Chapter Fifteen

It was Ray's first blind date. His suitor was a slightly older man with impressive life experience, a handsome bachelor but not a commitment phobe – and charming despite the slight hint of a belly and wonky set of lower teeth. I refused to entertain the thought that this match might not work out. Ray simply had to fall in love with Giggle.

Adam and I decided that it was best to do it on neutral territory, so they could have what dog experts refer to rather un-romantically as a 'brief sniff and move on'. We settled on the shady paths of Highgate Woods, where Rach had often taken Giggle for walks.

I headed past the play area, the scene of the most humiliating incident in my entire childhood. I must have been around ten years old when a stray dog grabbed my skirt by its hem and ripped it clean off, before disappearing into the woods with it dangling from its jaws. I had stood frozen to the spot in my striped knickers, hands crossed against my lower half, staring aghast at Rach. As at least thirty children collapsed with uncontrollable hysteria, booking my place in local history as 'the girl whose skirt was ripped off by a dog'. I smiled, looking at the shame monument, the Harold's arrow moment of my Bayeux tapestry with Rach.

I can't lie – the meeting with Giggle was not exactly the neat movie ending I'd fantasised about. They didn't run off into the open fields like twin canine souls as an orchestra performed 'Just the Two of Us'. Ray shivered by my legs while Adam tried to stop Giggle from crushing him with his over-enthusiasm. Giggle was also slightly thrown by the breathless rapture Ray's cuteness was inspiring in Mimi and her friends. He looked like a bewildered *Love Island* contestant struggling to cope with a bikini-clad newbie sashaying in to the villa. But Ray's curiosity slowly triumphed over his wariness, and a tentative sniffing session ensued.

'See, they're just getting used to each other,' said Mimi sensibly.

I took pictures on my phone, capturing the moment. I owed a huge debt of gratitude to this little chug with the funny teeth. Giggle had helped us through those chaotic first few months of grief. He had also shown me the sense of companionship and love that dogs can provide. There wouldn't have been a Ray if there hadn't been a Giggle.

'Does Ray love me more than everyone else?' asked Bertie, keen to establish the exact pecking order of this new social dynamic.

I was oddly fascinated by her question. It's one we start asking in childhood and go on to ask every day in adulthood, in slightly more artfully concealed ways. And the only answer we want is 'yes, it is you I love the most.' We throw ourselves into a space where our happiness relies on others. (Remember that bit where I told you I'd tried not to get irritatingly evangelical? I don't always manage it.)

I didn't tell Bertie any of this. It wouldn't have been an especially measured response to an amusing burst of six-year-old guilelessness. But for once I didn't just award her the prize of most cherished above all, as I once would have done.

'Ray loves all of us equally. He loves Mimi and me and Daddy and Giggle. He loves us all in different, wonderful ways. We all share his love. Isn't that nice?' I replied.

'Aw, that is SO nice,' she said with a slightly forced smile. 'But I really do think he does still love me *a little bit* the most.'

Look, we're all a work in progress.

Next on our list of doggy play dates were Katherine Ryan's three dogs, Dalai, Manny and Meg. We had discovered that by some weird coincidence, her Shih Tzu, Meg, had the same mother as Ray – the soap storyline none of us saw coming.

Dogs, as pack animals, don't really have any sense of biological recognition. So I wasn't expecting the reunion to go viral. But it was weird to see an almost obsessive display of devoted affection between them. Ray raced around after Meg, attacking her face with love bites and looking distraught if she left the room. Katherine's daughter, Violet, documented their relationship with endless photos, placing heart emojis and 'RAY RAY LOVES MEG!!' captions all over them.

'Do they know they are brother and sister, I wonder?' I asked Violet as they curled up together in the corner, looking like they were about to break the internet.

'I really think they do,' she said, of this live-action version of *Frozen* for dogs.

People kept telling me to take Ray to puppy classes (usually in slightly insistent tones after he'd peed on their carpet). I had resisted so far – I was worried that sensible ladies in fleeces would shout at me for giving Ray a girly hairstyle. And then there would be all those awkward dynamics that play out when strangers are thrown together over an unlikely commonality. But given that not too long ago I had chosen to enter a roomful of strangers wearing a label saying 'UNLOVEABLE', I couldn't hide behind that reason anymore.

I learned a very important lesson before I even set foot inside the class. Not everyone getting a dog was using it to deal with a load of unresolved childhood drama. Some people? They were literally just getting a dog.

The dog owners were milling around outside the class, indulging in the usual stilted getting-to-know-you formalities. Ray spotted a Cavapoo and gleefully lunged towards it. Its owner looked a bit like Anna Wintour, trench-coated and immaculate. She pulled angrily on the dog's expensive leather lead, as he inched towards Ray.

'Hello, gorgeous!' I said, bending down to stroke the Cavapoo. He pawed at my shins.

'Get DOWN!' Trench coat yelled at him. 'He is absolutely NOT allowed to leap up like that. It's the whole point of being here,' she sighed, thrusting sunglasses up on to her head to fix her dog with a death stare.

Lesson two. Not all dog owners were chatty, patient, open souls.

Inside, fortunately things were slightly less daunting. Louise, the trainer who had helped Ray with his agoraphobia and ran these classes, was here, wearing pink Converse and lime-green socks. I chatted to a couple with a dachshund named Peanut, and felt relieved that for once, Ray wouldn't have the shortest legs in the room (and neither would I). There was a girl with her boyfriend and their tiny chihuahua, and a cheery couple with a Labradoodle.

I was the only person who had come alone. I had to fight some reflexive discomfort over that. But I reminded myself that we were not in that world anymore. We tried to do things differently in this new place I'd moved to – my fancy new post-code called 'the present'.

We went round, rehab style, introducing our puppies and giving their ages. 'Ten weeks old,' one man said proudly. 'Twelve weeks old,' revealed a young couple. 'Sixteen weeks!' chuckled another owner. 'The old man of the group.'

Ray was not in increments of weeks anymore. He was eight months old. That made him thirty-two weeks. I'd brought a university graduate to a soft-play centre. I scanned quickly through the fact sheet I'd neglected to read. 'We prefer that puppies older than six months don't attend the classes,' it said, in unavoidable capitals.

'Emily? Do you want to introduce us to your dog?' Louise smiled.

'Absolutely! This is Raymond. He's . . . five months old! Well, five and a teeny bit, actually! Just a few days over . . .' I added, overcooking things needlessly, that old liar's tell.

But his dark secret allowed him to shine as the star pupil. As the other puppies misbehaved, Ray was a wise village elder. He looked slightly bewildered when I 'taught him' commands he had mastered some months back. 'I've kind of worked out the whole "treat as reward" concept by now? Talk about entry level, love.'

But the chaotic roomful of puppies made me look forward to the classes. Ray would waddle in, greeted like the well-loved sitcom character who receives whoops of approval from the studio audience.

'Bye, Ray Ray, we'll miss you!' a female couple said as they waved, heading off with their Schnoodle after the final session. 'Ray's such an angel.'

'Getting him is one of the best things I've ever done in my life,' I said.

For a second I reached for something funny to add, something self-deprecating and smart-mouthed that would hilariously dismantle the burst of sentiment.

But I stopped myself. Because it was true.

Chapter Sixteen

My house was crawling with Polish men.

Marek, Roland and Pavel were ripping out my old inherited bathroom and kitchen, painted in inoffensive neutral tones, to make way for my loud floor tiles and slightly in-your-face floral walls. I had also bought that pendant light that someone once declared to be 'a bit two years ago'.

I had approached this house renovation with the panic-stricken perfectionism of an oligarch's wedding planner. My poor builders nodded patiently as I commanded them to re-do the cupboard. 'It's come out a bit "surgical neck brace" pink. I'm thinking more "antique ballet slippers".' Assuming they would somehow be fluent in the Rach and Em shopping short-hand.

It was a revelation, just how satisfying it felt to create my own space from scratch. Those people who spent weekends piling plants and tap fittings into car boots had always been inhabitants of that other world as far as I was concerned. The proper adults, rather than the overgrown children like me. Ones whose shopping deliveries contained family-size packets of Andrex – not Prosecco and tooth-whitening kits. Homes were for dog families. Ray's bowls now had a fixed comforting place in the kitchen, and he went berserk when the cupboard door was opened, the portal to his theme park, filled with treats and toys.

'Raymond!' cried Pavel as Ray scuttled around threatening to knock over a bucket of cement. 'You will be like dog statue. Leave, shoo!'

Marek, the youngest builder, smirked, replying to him in Polish as he sucked on endless cigarettes.

I had grown oddly fond of Marek's enigmatic daily musings.

'Isn't my niece cute, Marek?' I would say.

'All children are cute,' he replied.

Or, 'I telephone my uncle now, Emily.'

'The one I met the other day, Marek?'

'Different one.'

'How many uncles have you got?'

'Forty.'

Or, 'Marek, did you want this mug?'

'It's cup.'

'Actually, it's called a mug!'

'Hmmm. We'll see.'

Getting the builders in to do up your house probably didn't count as a hugely symbolic moment for most people. It was just something they quietly got on with throughout their lives, as circumstances demanded and money allowed.

But it felt weighted with huge significance to me. I had never had the courage to put my own stamp on anything.

The two homes I'd bought so far had come tastefully but neutrally pre-prepared, so that I didn't have to disagree with the previous owner and their confident decisions about the best way to live. I would add the occasional print or a cushion that a colleague or interiors magazine had already given the seal of approval. People told me, 'You have such great taste, Em!' as I rushed to place flowers on the table and wiped toothpaste stains off the bathroom mirror so that they would leave with an impression of perfection. But I didn't care how it looked when they left. Until now.

I bought a huge French-style bed that made me feel like Marie Antoinette, and hung up the last Christmas present Rach bought me, a beautiful illustration of a peach, bought on one of her east London market visits.

There was a baroque white frame in my living room that used to contain a picture of me laughing, at a movie premiere. I took it out. I swapped it with a letter I wrote at the age of six.

Dear mummy, try and understand what I'm telling you. Rach makes me giggle and then you tell me off. It sounds silly but it's true. Love Emmy xxxx

As important documents went, it probably wasn't up there with Gandhi's letter to Hitler, 'Friends have been asking me to write to you today for the sake of humanity.' But I liked the oddness of this scrappy torn-off child's note inside a grand ornate frame. It was exactly the kind of unorthodox detail that would once have decorated my childhood home. And the note managed to sum up the family script I had stuck to for so long. Me casting myself as hapless victim of a hopelessly corrupt justice system, Mum partisan judge unable to control her emotional responses, Rach golden favourite. And Dad, as ever, absent from it all.

I tried not to see any of us like that anymore.

But mostly, the note just really made me laugh.

The renovations meant that I finally had to clear out and wade through my family's old things, which were shoved away in bags and cases piled on top of each other, a jumble of memories that had felt too overwhelming to tackle until now.

I started with my father's books. I had kept a handful of them, including his well-thumbed copies of Philip Larkin and TS Eliot, with scribbles and underlines in the margins. There was an Ian McEwan novel, the first page of which featured my father's handwritten scrawl, his writing spidery with age. 'McEwan severs heads with exquisitely good taste!'

He used to do that a lot, write things about literary strengths and weaknesses in a book, like those handwritten staff reviews in Waterstones. Not as a way of remembering something that spoke to him. It was more as if he was desperately trying to engage the author in debate, vaguely recalling a time when he could swear he had those kinds of conversations in real life.

There were yellowing cuttings of his glory years, all preserved in scrapbooks by my mum, who was fastidious when it came to preserving our archive. I looked through letters from Gore Vidal and Harold Pinter, as well as *Times* features I had never bothered to read before. There was an old tabloid article about his now forgotten moment as the first man on British colour TV.

Some small picture frames were buried at the bottom of one of his cases. There was a photo of Rach sitting on a wicker chair stroking Mimi's sleepy head, and one of my grandfather blinking at the sun in his beret. And then I spotted a picture of me. I must have been about three years old, dressed in a pink velvet dress, tomato stains on my chin, reaching across to plant a kiss on his face. I hadn't noticed it in his flat when I was clearing everything out, placing it in bin bags. Perhaps pride had prevented him from putting it on show.

I found a stack of postcards that he'd sent Rach and me during his absences over the years. He would often sign off with a piece of advice. Sometimes it was a subtle reference to things going on that Mum had obviously told him about. Discreet afterthoughts that he dropped in, aware that he'd relinquished the right to offer direct parental advice.

'Every day is a new beginning and a different kind of failure.'

'Be wary of people who make more noise than impact.'

'Never shed a single salt tear for this departed year. Embrace the crunch of jackboots marching in triumph over its ignominious grave.'

'Mutual stubbornness can become a war of silence. The older wiser person must end the stalemate.'

I assumed that last one had been an attempt to help resolve some teenage dispute between Rach and me. It felt strange reading it now, given my very own stalemate with him that had denied us a resolution. Perhaps it had been softened slightly, with that brief final glance he gave me.

I felt a sense of pride, for the first time, looking through these fragments of his exceptional mind. And love. He was undeniably guilty of a lot of things, my dad. But as I'd learned on my week in Ireland, all of us are guilty in our different ways. And none of us are completely to blame.

There were huge boxes of all my mum's old photos. Her and Dad starting out on their ill-fated union, with smiles and knee-high boots. Her hopeful glow dwindled in later snapshots, as she juggled children with a man there by accident rather than design. I found several volumes of diaries containing funny things Rach and I had said and detailed descriptions of dinner parties. As well as more painful feelings, highlighting the gulf between the life she longed for and the one she'd chosen with my father. I wanted to give her a huge hug.

There were entries referring to 'hours at the bloody Nigerian embassy picking up my SODDING mother. Pissed of course.' The protest Rach and I left in her bed to sabotage a night of passion. 'The girls left talcum powder, a Tampax wrapper and a drawing pin for me and John tonight – little bastards!!!' I found the notebook entitled MIMI'S SAYINGS, its pages filled with her observations. It stopped suddenly the month Rach got her diagnosis. Just a bunch of empty pages, which told a story all of their own.

My mum had kept all our school reports (although why anyone would archive 'Emily is totally at sea in mathematics and does little to help herself' beats me) as well as all the notes Rach and I left each other. 'Borrowed ya top Em – DON'T BE CROSS PLSE!!'

I looked through the glittery birthday cards that said 'WORLD'S BEST SISTER!' and a stack of photos labelled 'RACH AND EM'. There was one of us posing by a movie poster for *Sister Act* at Leicester Square tube, my mother art directing us off camera, as we adopted the tight smiles of hostages in propaganda photos. Rach and I dancing together on her wedding day to Kylie's 'Spinning Around', drunk on joy (in her case) and vodka (mine).

The Life-Changing Magic of Tidying firmly advises chucking out stuff like this. You're meant to edit all your memories into one organised box file. But I decided to flagrantly disregard this advice and put it all in floral boxes for Mimi and Bertie. I hoped they would look through it together one day, and relate to a memory of Rach, not as an angelic myth but as a complex person with a textured backstory – and flaws. She could be overly defensive when criticised, never did have enough faith in her creative talent and was a terrible gossip. She was prone to the occasional fashion mistake, (hello, turquoise silk shirt with diamanté collar), disastrous romance (the man forever known as 'That AWFUL bloke') and had an utterly misplaced confidence in her ability to sing 'Me and Mrs Jones' in the right key.

But I wanted her girls to have their very own tapestry of her life, one that they could get to know gradually, in all its gloriously unvarnished detail.

Cookie Monster had been right to warn me all those years ago. My family was hopelessly, unavoidably, wilfully not like the others. But the stupid blue acrylic fool had forgotten to tell me the most important thing: that was what made them so impossible to forget. I didn't hear him belting out any songs dedicated to 'Those Things Like Everything Else'.

It had taken me a long time to realise that the dog-family kingdom I'd longed to join simply didn't exist. The idyllic marriage, the golden child, the obedient Labrador – it was all just scenery, an alternative backdrop for the same messy chaos that played out in everyone's lives.

My family weren't around anymore but they had left me with a sense of where I belonged. It was a place where you were allowed to be a little strange. Where no one cared if you took a different path to everyone else. The funny world where the people not-quite-like-the-others lived. I was happy to come home.

Epilogue

The Gothic entrance gates clanged as they shut behind us. This wasn't how I'd envisaged introducing my loving hero to my sister and my parents. Him hiding from cemetery staff in a straw tote bag with a bone-shaped treat in his mouth, about to greet three tombstones. But let's face it, my own meet-the-parents moment never was going to follow the traditional form.

The sun scattered light through the cedar trees overhanging the paths that took us to my family's respective resting places. There was a guided tour being shown around, and I watched the group being led to the resting places of writers and artists and a famous Russian spy. They listened attentively to the guide talking about mausoleums and then a couple caught my eye, conscious suddenly that this historical place had a more intimate significance for visitors clutching flowers and cloths for wiping down headstones.

But it wasn't poignant memories that were overwhelming me at this point – more panicked fear that Ray would poke his head above the straw bag, revealing his illegal presence. I imagined the guide dramatically interrupting the gentle Sunday tour, leading Ray and me away shamefaced, as he said into a two-way radio, 'Suspect apprehended near grave of George Michael's mother. Currently detained in Top Shop raffia shoulder bag. Back-up requested.'

I turned away from the tour party, adopting what I hoped was the body language of someone requiring privacy, rather than a woman concealing a contraband Shih Tzu. They discreetly took their leave and five minutes later I felt safe enough to liberate Ray. He chose to mark this moment by cocking his tiny leg against a collapsing angel on a Victorian tomb.

I clambered up the grassy bank to where my sister lies, and wiped off some bird poo from the limestone block. The words had been subdued by the battle scars of weather, but you could still make out the inscription my brother-in-law chose for her legacy: 'Full of Life and Love'.

'Hey, Rach. So guess what? I finally got a dog. And I called him Ray, kind of after you. I hope you don't think that's weird.'

Ray was just wrapping up a toilet break. He had adopted that oddly heartbreaking expression that characterises dogs' bathroom sessions – vulnerability with a dash of dignity.

'Come on, Ray! Come and see Rach!' I called out.

He ran, pink tongue dangling out, glossy fur flying, eyes wild with excitement as his tiny legs stumbled up the bank and he settled at my feet, sniffing the faded pink roses I had placed in a little glass bottle.

'Ray, meet Ray,' I said, smiling suddenly at the utter absurdity of what I was doing – formally introducing a dead sister to a

Shih Tzu. But she would have got it. That was the thing about Rach – she always did.

You can't alter how your story begins, but you can write the ending any way you like.

I hadn't had the usual kind of journey. And the male hero who managed to save me was a little different to the regular romcom kind. But perhaps I had managed to get my uplifting movie ending after all. The one I had written all myself.

An invitation from the publisher

Join us at www.hodder.co.uk, or follow us
on Twitter @hodderbooks to be a part of
our community of people who love the very
best in books and reading.

Whether you want to discover more about a book
or an author, watch trailers and interviews, have the
chance to win early limited editions, or simply browse
our expert readers' selection of the very best books,
we think you'll find what you're looking for.

And if you don't, that's the place to tell us what's missing.

We love what we do, and we'd love you to be a part of it.

www.hodder.co.uk

@hodderbooks

HodderBooks

HodderBooks